# Contents

# THE
# HARVARD MEDICAL
# SCHOOL GUIDE TO
# HEALING YOUR
# SINUSES

## RALPH B. METSON, M.D.

### WITH STEVEN MARDON

**McGraw·Hill**

New York   Chicago   San Francisco   Lisbon   London   Madrid   Mexico City
Milan   New Delhi   San Juan   Seoul   Singapore   Sydney   Toronto

1  2  3  4  5  6  7  8  9  0    DOC/DOC    0  9  8  7  6  5

ISBN 0-07-144469-6

Interior design by Think Design Group, LLC
Interior artwork by Robert Galla
Images on pages 39, 71, 141, and 142 courtesy of Ralph Metson

McGraw-Hill books are available at special quantity discounts to use as premiums and sales promotions, or for use in corporate training programs. For more information, please write to the Director of Special Sales, Professional Publishing, McGraw-Hill, Two Penn Plaza, New York, NY 10121-2298. Or contact your local bookstore.

The information contained in this book is intended to provide helpful and informative material on the subject addressed. It is not intended to serve as a replacement for professional medical advice. Any use of the information in this book is at the reader's discretion. The author, publisher, and the President and Fellows of Harvard College specifically disclaim any and all liability arising directly or indirectly from the use or application of any information contained in this book. A health care professional should be consulted regarding your specific situation.

This book is printed on acid-free paper.

*To Taren*

# Preface

It's amazing how few books have been written about sinusitis. Considering the millions of people who suffer from sinusitis each year, you'd think that there would be volumes in every bookstore, not to mention frequent magazine and newspaper articles on the topic. I first realized the need for such a book when Judy Foreman, a syndicated health columnist, interviewed me for an article on nasal irrigations for sinusitis. Judy later informed me that she received more e-mail in response to that piece than to any column she had written in years.

But the truth is that for most people, including journalists and doctors, sinusitis elicits neither the excitement of a new medical breakthrough nor the drama of a life-threatening illness. Besides, most people with sinusitis *do* get better. But what about those who don't? I'm referring to the millions of people with chronic infections whose headaches and drainage and congestion keep returning despite repeated courses of medications. I'm talking about individuals who wander from doctor to doctor seeking some sort of relief and others who suffer in silence. Those are the people for whom *Healing Your Sinuses* was written.

This book contains more than just a collection of facts. It reflects a philosophy I've developed over the past two decades treating patients with sinus disorders. My goal was to write a book about sinusitis that was concise yet covered all the essential topics, that was based on scientific fact yet included my opinion on what treatments I thought were best, and that discussed the latest technical advances yet gave simple, practical advice on how to get relief from common symptoms.

You might say that being a sinus specialist is in my blood. My great-uncle, who graduated from medical school in 1900, was one of the first ear, nose, and throat (ENT) specialists in the country, and my father recently retired as an ENT physician after fifty-one years of practice. When I completed my specialty training at UCLA in 1985, I joined the staff at the Massachusetts Eye and Ear Infirmary and the faculty of Harvard Medical School at the same time that revolutionary new theories about sinusitis were being developed.

The unique academic environment at Harvard enabled me to develop a clinical and research practice in which I applied these new ideas to the treatment of patients who had sinus problems. My research endeavors have focused on three main areas: the impact of sinusitis on quality of life; the development of new techniques, including lasers, to treat sinusitis; and the introduction of computer navigation systems to enhance the safety and efficacy of sinus surgery. One of my greatest pleasures has been the opportunity to share my ideas and skills with medical students, residents, and fellows whom I teach on a daily basis.

During the past twenty years, I've had the privilege of treating thousands of patients who have entrusted me with their care. Whether their noses were blocked, their sense of smell was gone, or their sinuses just couldn't drain, I've tried to combine the art and science of medicine to provide relief. The writing of this book represents my first attempt to reach beyond the scope of my practice and communicate directly with the large community of individuals who suffer from sinusitis. It is my sincere desire that by doing so, you and many others like you will be able to discover the key to healing your sinuses.

# Acknowledgments

This book would never have been written were it not for the influence of the first ear, nose, and throat (ENT) doctor I ever met—my father, Bates F. Metson, M.D., who, along with my mother, Petty Metson, has served as a lifelong role model. I still remember making rounds with my dad when I was a boy, looking up to him and to his head mirror and hoping to wear one myself someday.

During my more formal medical education, I was blessed to have many great teachers, including Dr. Paul Ward and Dr. Vicente Honrubia at UCLA Medical School. They inspired me to pursue a career in academic medicine, where I could find fulfillment through the proper balance of clinical care, research, and teaching.

After moving to Boston, I was fortunate to encounter two additional mentors: Dr. Harold Schuknecht and Dr. William Montgomery. Both of these distinguished physicians educated me and a generation of otolaryngologists at Harvard Medical School.

I would also like to thank my current colleagues at the Massachusetts Eye and Ear Infirmary, particularly Dr. Joseph B. Nadol Jr. and Dr. Richard Gliklich, whose advice and support have been invaluable to my medical career.

A parallel career of a different sort has been that of my expanding family, including my three daughters—Vered, born during internship; Danielle, born during residency; and Jenna, born during fellowship—and my son-in-law Michael, who joined us during professorship. They, along with my parents-in-law,

Dr. Norman and Lela Jacoby, serve as a constant source of encouragement and keep me focused on the important things in life.

This book was a team effort, and I would like to acknowledge the critical assistance of a key player on that team, my cowriter, Steven Mardon. I would also like to thank my editors—Judith McCarthy from McGraw-Hill and Nancy Ferrari and Dr. Tony Komaroff from Harvard Health Publications—who shepherded this book from its inception to its printing. The original illustrations in this book reflect the talent of medical illustrator Robert Galla.

Finally, a word of thanks to my manuscript readers and contributors, whose feedback and suggestions greatly enhanced the quality of this book: syndicated health columnist Judy Foreman; my current Rhinology Fellow Dr. Stacey Gray; and my wife, Taren Metson, whose love and support guide me in all that I do.

PART I

# The Sinuses in Health and Disease

# CHAPTER 1

# Sinusitis and Quality of Life

It's a simple but revealing question: compared to one year ago, how would you rate your health today?

I frequently ask this question to patients who have been referred to me with sinusitis, and nearly always their answer is: worse. If you're struggling with sinus problems, chances are you would say the same.

What's important about this response is it reflects that sinusitis leads to more than just headaches or nasal drainage or blocked breathing passages. It affects your overall quality of life. Regardless of your worst symptom—whether it's pain, congestion, a perpetually runny nose, fatigue, or something else—you share a common bond with others who have sinusitis: reduced quality of life. Basic elements of daily living—from getting a good night's sleep to doing your job to enjoying your free time—may become difficult or impossible.

That's the bad news. Fortunately, there's good news about sinusitis, too—enough to fill several chapters in this book, and I hope enough to help you find long-lasting relief. But before you dig in, I'd like to start by raising a few key points.

## You Are Not Alone

You have plenty of company in experiencing sinus problems. Chronic sinusitis (see the sidebar "Defining Sinusitis") is one of the most commonly diagnosed chronic illnesses in the United States, more prevalent than heart disease and migraine headaches. More than thirty-five million adult Americans suffered from sinusitis in 2001, according to a 2004 report by the U.S. Centers for Disease Control and Prevention. That's a whopping 17.4 percent of American adults. Table 1.1 shows you where sinusitis fits in among other commonly diagnosed chronic diseases.

Here are some key sinusitis statistics:

- Americans make nearly 800,000 emergency department visits annually for sinusitis.
- Sinusitis causes Americans to miss about twenty-five million workdays a year.

**TABLE 1.1** Number of Americans with Chronic Diseases

| Disease | # in Millions |
|---|---|
| Lower back pain | 63.2 |
| Hypertension | 41.8 |
| Arthritis | 41.2 |
| **Sinusitis** | 35.5 |
| Neck pain | 34.0 |
| Migraines/ severe headaches | 33.9 |
| Heart disease | 23.5 |
| Asthma | 22.2 |
| Hay fever | 20.4 |
| Stomach ulcers | 18.9 |
| Diabetes | 13.0 |

Source: CDC. Summary Health Statistics for U.S. Adults: National Health Interview Survey, 2001. January 2004.

## Defining Sinusitis

The simplest definition of *sinusitis* comes from its Latin roots. The common medical suffix *itis* means "inflammation of," so sinusitis is an inflammation of the sinuses.

Because most people whose sinuses are inflamed also experience inflammation of the nose, some physicians now use the term *rhinosinusitis* in place of *sinusitis*. (*Rhino* means "nose" in Greek.) I'm not crazy about this term because I think it unnecessarily complicates matters, but you may encounter it.

- Americans spend $2 billion annually for over-the-counter medications for nasal and sinus disorders and about $200 million on prescription medications for sinusitis.
- People with sinus problems undergo more than 460,000 sinus surgeries each year in the United States, making it one of the most commonly performed surgical procedures.

These numbers are up from a decade ago, and health experts expect further increases in the future. Possibly due to pollution and other factors, the prevalence of all breathing-related ailments—not just sinusitis, but also allergies and asthma—is rising and shows no signs of leveling off.

And not only is chronic sinusitis common, it strikes people during their most productive years. It's far more likely to occur between the ages of twenty and sixty-five than during childhood or teen years or late in life. And it affects people in all walks of life: teachers, police officers, nurses . . . even U.S. presidents (see the sidebar "FDR and Sinusitis").

## Sinusitis Is a Serious Problem

Sinusitis keeps a low profile. Despite its prevalence, you don't often read about it in the newspaper. It's rarely fatal, so it lacks a dramatic hook for most nightly news programs. Sinusitis is so

## FDR and Sinusitis

Most people are aware that President Franklin Delano Roosevelt used a wheelchair following a bout with polio in his thirties. What's less well known is that FDR also suffered from chronic sinusitis. In his childhood and adolescence, FDR frequently experienced respiratory ailments (such as sinusitis, sore throats, and bronchitis), according to *The Hidden Campaign: FDR's Health and the 1944 Election*, by Hugh E. Evans, M.D. These problems continued throughout his adult life. FDR's personal physician during his presidency, Vice Admiral Ross McIntire, was likely chosen for the post because he was an ear, nose, and throat (ENT) specialist who was best suited to treat recurrent sinus infections.

unfamiliar to the general public that people who talk about their discomfort risk being labeled as complainers. My patients frequently tell me, "Nobody understands just how miserable this is," when describing how their symptoms make them feel.

In fact, I heard this comment so often that a few years ago, I decided to do a scientific study of the effect sinusitis has on quality of life. For four years my colleagues at Harvard Medical School and I tracked 150 patients, comparing them to a similar group of patients with other chronic problems, such as heart disease and back pain.

Even though I treat sinusitis patients every day, I was still surprised by the results. People with chronic sinusitis reported the highest levels of pain among the diseases we compared, which included heart disease, lower back pain, and chronic lung disease. They also fared the worst on tests of social functioning, a measure of the extent health interferes with normal social activities. And our study found sinusitis had a significant effect on individuals' work life, energy, and mental health.

Other researchers have since made similar findings. So if you feel like nobody believes you, I want you to know: I believe you, and I've written this book to help you and millions of others with sinus problems like yours.

## Diagnosis and Treatment Have Improved Dramatically

Much has happened in recent decades to make it easier to diagnose and treat sinusitis. Until the early 1980s, physicians had a hard time just identifying sinusitis. X-rays, the most common diagnostic tool, were not precise enough to detect small sinus blockages. Only those people with the most severe obstructions, such as large polyps, had abnormal x-ray findings. So patients with sinusitis often were misdiagnosed as having migraine headaches or were told they had nothing at all, leaving them untreated and extremely frustrated.

Two major technological developments have greatly improved our ability to diagnose sinus disease. First, we now have endoscopes (thin telescopes with high-resolution optics), which a doctor can pass through the nostrils to closely inspect the sinus drainage passages. Second, old-fashioned x-rays have been supplanted by CT scans, a radiological tool that enables us to get a highly detailed and accurate image of the inside of a patient's sinuses.

Even more significantly, treatments for sinusitis have vastly improved. More options exist and they are easier for patients to obtain. A large variety of devices for irrigating and cleaning the sinuses are now available in most drugstores. You can order a mist machine called a nebulizer, which delivers medications such as antibiotics or antifungal agents in high concentrations directly into the sinuses, where they can be most effective. And new and more powerful antibiotics are now available. So when you have a sinus infection, your doctor can choose from an antibiotic arsenal more likely to quickly rid your body of invading bacteria.

For those select people who do not improve with sinus irrigations or medications, developments in sinus surgery over the past two decades have been nothing short of revolutionary. In years past, sinus surgery was a major ordeal involving incisions on the face or through the gums under the upper lip. The procedures often literally left patients black and blue, and recovery could be prolonged. Patients' noses often had to be packed with six-foot-long gauze strips, forcing them to breathe exclusively through their mouths for up to a week, and removing the packing was painful.

Thankfully, those days are over.

New techniques pioneered in the 1980s and refined in the 1990s allow surgeons to enter the sinuses directly through the nose and remove nasal obstructions with extreme precision, while leaving healthy adjacent tissue untouched. To do this, we use endoscopes that can be attached to lasers or tiny shavers that rotate several thousand times a minute. And navigational tracking systems in the operating room now work like Global Positioning Systems, allowing surgeons to track the precise location of their surgical instruments within the sinuses on a three-dimensional computer monitor. This technology helps reduce the risk of a surgical error that might injure the eye or brain, causing blindness or stroke. With computer-assisted technology, sinus surgery is now usually done on an outpatient basis, and packing typically needs to stay in just one night or isn't necessary at all.

I'll discuss these treatment options—and many others—in greater depth later in the book. For now, perhaps you can take comfort in knowing that effective treatment is available when you need it.

## You Can—and Should—Play an Active Role in Your Treatment

With some medical conditions, treatment is controlled by the physician, leaving the patient with little to do but take medication and hope for the best. Chronic sinusitis is not one of those conditions. Numerous treatment options exist, and what works best will depend on your history, symptoms, personality, and lifestyle. I often tell my patients, "You are your own best advocate."

## What's Next

To serve yourself effectively, you need an understanding of the ABCs of sinusitis. So this book's first few chapters will give you the basics on the anatomy and function of your sinuses, the distinction between acute and chronic sinusitis, and the different factors that might be causing your sinusitis. You'll need that fundamental knowledge as we move on in subsequent chapters to cover the range of available sinusitis treatments, starting with the simplest and moving to the most advanced, as shown in Figure 1.1.

One final point: these days you see a lot of medical hyperbole in the media. While there is genuine cause for optimism, I cannot promise that you will be cured if you read this book and follow my recommendations (although some people may be).

**FIGURE 1.1** Stepwise Approach to Sinusitis Treatment

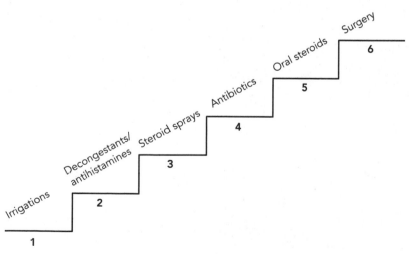

*The stepwise approach to sinusitis starts with the simplest treatments first and progresses, if necessary, to the most advanced treatments.*

Unfortunately, sinusitis tends to be a chronic condition. But here are some realistic improvements you can expect:

- If you've averaged five to ten courses of antibiotics each year for your sinusitis, you may find that with proper treatment you'll only need two or three courses in coming years.
- If you suffer from thick, troublesome postnasal drip, you may discover the drainage is thinner, reducing the need to constantly clear your throat or blow your nose.
- If you have chronic congestion, you may notice yourself breathing easier when you exercise or lie down at night.

Even more important, you'll see quality of life improvements, such as reduced sick days, higher energy, and better mental health. It's not uncommon for patients I've treated to tell me they feel like a whole new person.

# CHAPTER 2

# How Your Sinuses Work

Before you can understand how to treat the things that can go wrong with your sinuses, you have to know what the sinuses are and how healthy sinuses work. We're about to embark on a journey through the human anatomy that will be a little like the 1960s movie *Fantastic Voyage*, except your destination as a miniaturized traveler is the nasal passages instead of the brain, and I'm sorry to have to say that the actress Raquel Welch is nowhere to be found.

## Entering the Nasal House: Your Nose as the Foyer

I like to think of the sinuses as existing inside a home—call it the Nasal House. The house has two big doors—your nostrils—and they're always open.

Like many houses, the outside doors lead to a foyer. In the Nasal House, the foyer is your nose. Let's take a look at the interior of your nose.

Your nose is mostly made of cartilage (tough elastic tissue) and bone. The tip (the part you can wiggle if you pinch it with your fingers) is made of cartilage, and the bridge (where a person's glasses rest) is made of bone.

Your nose is divided into two roughly equal-sized halves by a thin partition called the septum. Made of flexible cartilage in front and bone in back, the septum is typically about three to four inches long. In Chapter 18, I'll discuss the consequences of having a septum that's crooked (a deviated septum) and how this problem can be corrected.

## The Nasal Cavity: A Hallway with a Climate Control System

Next on our tour, you see that the back of the foyer opens into a long, narrow hallway—the nasal cavity. About halfway down this hallway, you see a series of doors, each of which opens into a different room. The rooms are your sinuses, and there are four pairs of them.

The first doors you see on your left and right lead to the maxillary sinuses, located in your cheeks. A little farther along, you come to the doors to the ethmoid sinuses, located between your eyes. Next, you see two doors leading upward, as if to an attic; those are the doors to the frontal sinuses, in your forehead. And the last pair of doors you see at the very far end of the hallway lead to the sphenoid sinuses, behind your nose. Figures 2.1 and 2.2 show the location of the sinuses.

## What's the Difference Between *Mucus* and *Mucous*?

It's a matter of language—they refer to the same thing, but *mucus* is a noun and *mucous* is an adjective.

So *mucus* is the actual slippery substance inside your nose and sinuses. It gets its name from *mucin*, the molecule that is its primary component.

*Mucous*, meanwhile, is the word that describes a number of things related to mucus. The most important is mucous membrane, a thin sheet rich in the glands that secrete mucus. Mucous membranes (also known as mucosa, for short) are not unique to the lining of the nose and sinuses; they also line much of the respiratory and digestive tracts.

**FIGURE 2.1** Location of the Sinuses

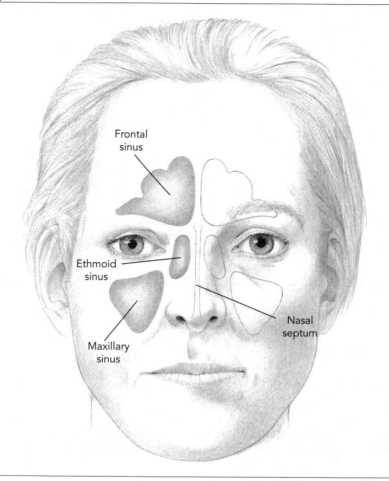

Frontal
sinus

Ethmoid
sinus

Maxillary
sinus

Nasal
septum

*The frontal sinuses are located in the forehead, the ethmoid sinuses are between the eyes, and the maxillary sinuses are behind the cheeks.*

Unlike most real houses, the doors in the Nasal House are not big and rectangular. Instead, they're round, like something you'd see in a hobbit's home in *The Lord of the Rings*, and very tiny— about the size of a pinhole. They are called ostia. In a healthy person, the ostia usually stay open, allowing air to move in and out freely and mucus to drain from the sinuses (see the sidebar "What's the Difference Between *Mucus* and *Mucous*?"). But if

13

**FIGURE 2.2** Inside the Nose

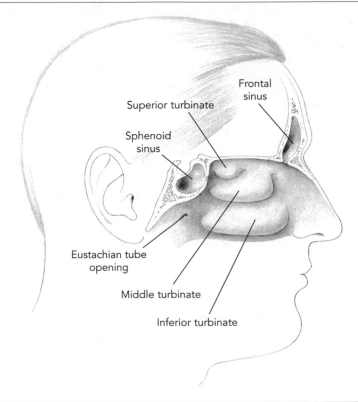

Frontal sinus

Superior turbinate

Sphenoid sinus

Eustachian tube opening

Middle turbinate

Inferior turbinate

*The sphenoid sinus located behind the nose is shown on this side view. The inferior, middle, and superior turbinates, which run the length of the nasal cavity, serve to warm and humidify inhaled air. The opening to the Eustachian tube, which equalizes pressure in the ear, can be seen just behind the turbinates.*

there's trouble—such as swelling from infection or allergies—the ostia close, and the rooms tend to get stale and stuffy inside.

As you know, your nose serves as a pathway for air to enter and leave the lungs. You breathe in oxygen (along with nitrogen and other gases) and breathe out carbon dioxide. You could do this exclusively through your mouth, but if you did, problems would soon arise: your mouth would get dry, and you would breathe in dust particles floating in the air, which would make you cough a lot.

An amazing internal climate control system in the Nasal House enables you to avoid these problems. The key to climate control is the turbinates, large bones that act as the Nasal House's equivalent of radiators. As you stroll down the hallway, you see three pairs of these radiator-like structures along the walls of the nasal cavity: a large pair near the floor (the inferior turbinates), a smaller pair above them (the middle turbinates), and an even smaller pair hanging from the ceiling (the superior turbinates). Figure 2.2 shows the turbinates.

The inferior turbinates are typically about three inches long, the middle turbinates are half as long, and the superior turbinates are shorter still. If you look into your nostrils with a flashlight in front of a mirror, you can actually see the tips of the inferior turbinates. They look like pink, shiny mounds along the sides of the nose.

The turbinates serve three important roles in preparing air for the lungs: they provide warmth, humidification, and filtration. How does this three-in-one climate control system work?

- **Heat.** The turbinates function like a household hot-water radiator system, except they use circulating blood instead of water. Each turbinate is completely covered by a spongelike membrane through which blood continuously flows. So the warm blood heats the incoming air. Interestingly, about every six hours, blood flow increases on one side of the nose and decreases on the other as this spongy lining expands and contracts (see the sidebar "The Nasal Cycle").
- **Humidification.** Inhaled air flows over each turbinate's membrane, which is not only warm but moist. Microscopic droplets of watery fluid and mucus are constantly secreted along the membrane's surface into the air. If you were to linger in this part of the Nasal House, you would probably say it feels like a sauna. To get an idea of how much moisture is contained in nasal air, you need only hold a mirror beneath your nostrils and watch it quickly fog up as you exhale.

## The Nasal Cycle

You've probably noticed how at times you breathe through only one side of the nose, while the other side is blocked. You may have thought there was a problem, but this nasal cycle is actually very normal. Through sleep and wakefulness, the dominant side for breathing switches back and forth about four times a day.

The nasal cycle exists because the blood supply to the mucous membranes in the nose fluctuates. About every six hours, blood flow increases on one side of the nose and decreases on the other. The side where it's increased swells and does a little more air warming, while the side where blood flow decreases opens up and does a little more of the breathing.

- **Filtration.** The membrane's inherent stickiness from its thin coating of mucus enables it to snare unwanted particles you breathe in and prevent them from traveling to the lungs.

All three of these functions are enhanced by the scroll shape of the turbinates, which greatly enhances their surface area.

Taken as a whole, the Nasal House's climate control system is a model of efficiency. It ensures that the nasal cavity is not just any hallway with stale air; it's a hallway with precisely treated air, optimally conditioned for the lungs.

## The OMC: A Critical Passageway

There is one final critical piece of anatomy in the Nasal House I've yet to mention—a narrow turnstile in the hallway through which you must pass before you reach the sinus doors. This turnstile is a common point of entry in and out of the sinuses. But it can also serve as a bottleneck. If the turnstile becomes blocked, nothing can get in or out of the sinuses—not air, not mucus. This

**FIGURE 2.3** Location of the OMC

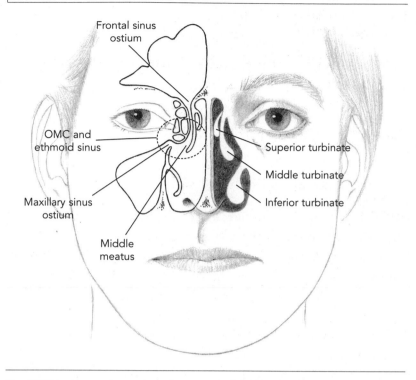

The OMC (ostiomeatal complex), shown on the left side of this diagram, serves as a common drainage pathway for the frontal, ethmoid, and maxillary sinuses. The location of the turbinates, which attach to the side walls of the nose, is also shown. Note the proximity of the OMC to the middle turbinate, which can cause sinus obstruction if it becomes enlarged.

turnstile has a name: the ostiomeatal complex, or OMC for short. *Ostio* refers to the small doors, or ostia, of each sinus, and *meatal* refers to the middle meatus—the area adjacent to the middle turbinate, in which the OMC is located. In the Nasal House, there are actually three meatuses—inferior, middle, and superior—each located adjacent to the turbinate of the same name. Figure 2.3 shows the OMC.

It sounds technical, but it's worth remembering because the OMC plays a critical role in healthy sinus function. Many sinus problems can be traced to obstructions in the OMC, and you'll be hearing more about it in coming chapters.

## A House with Eight Rooms: Your Four Pairs of Sinuses

Now that you're familiar with the major anatomical structures in the nasal cavity, let's take a look inside each of the four pairs of sinuses.

### Ethmoid

We'll start with the ethmoid sinuses—which are located behind the bridge of your nose, between your eyes—because they are in many ways the most important. You might think of the ethmoid sinuses as the gatekeepers of the Nasal House. That's because the frontal and maxillary sinuses first drain through the ethmoid sinuses before reaching the nose. So if your ethmoid sinuses are not draining properly, then your other sinuses are likely to get clogged as well.

The ethmoid sinuses differ from the maxillary, frontal, and sphenoid sinuses in one key respect: they are not single, large chambers. Instead, each ethmoid sinus comprises five to ten little chambers, separated by very thin-walled bones and lined with mucous membranes (see Figure 2.3). Each of these chambers has its own separate small drainage opening into the nasal cavity. Even with so many chambers, the ethmoid sinuses are usually the smallest sinuses. They are about the shape and size of a matchbox.

### Maxillary

The maxillary sinuses are the cheek sinuses. They are located behind your cheekbones, extending from just beneath your eyes to just above your upper teeth. In fact, the roots of the teeth of the upper jaw often protrude into the floor of the maxillary sinuses, which is why many people with sinus infections have tooth pain. The maxillary sinuses are usually the first sinuses to develop in the womb (see the sidebar "Are We Born with

## Are We Born with Sinuses?

Children don't have all their sinuses when they're born. They have rudimentary maxillary and ethmoid sinuses, but their frontal and sphenoid sinuses are usually absent. Frontal sinuses typically develop by age eight, and sphenoid sinuses develop by age twelve.

Sinuses?"). They're usually triangular in shape and about the size of a large walnut.

### Frontal

The frontal sinuses are the forehead sinuses. They're located within the frontal bone of your forehead. The back wall of the frontal sinuses actually forms the bone overlying the brain. The size of the frontal sinuses can vary greatly from one person to another. People with large frontal sinuses generally have large brows. Interestingly, about 10 percent of the population never develops frontal sinuses. We have no idea why, and people without frontal sinuses don't seem to miss them.

### Sphenoid

The sphenoid sinuses might be considered the deep sinuses. They're located in the back part of the nose, deep within the skull, positioned in a delicate location where the eyes and brain meet. Each sphenoid sinus is about the size of a large grape. The carotid artery, a major artery that carries blood to the brain, runs through the outer walls of the sphenoid sinus. In fact, a surgeon looking inside your sphenoid sinuses sometimes can see the carotid artery pulsating when the overlying bone is thin.

## Inside Your Sinuses: Mucus, Cilia, and Glands

Now it's time for the final phase of our journey—through the doors and right into your sinuses. It's a jarring sight.

Once inside a sinus, you immediately notice a strange, textured wallpaper on all the walls. It is rough and sticky to the touch, with hundreds of small bumps on the surface that look like chocolate chips breaking through the crust of a cookie. On close inspection, you also observe thousands of tiny hairs that look like fine fiber threads completely covering the wallpaper surface.

The bumps are mucus-secreting glands, and they do exactly what their name suggests. The mucus produced by these glands coats the lining of the entire sinus interior, creating a sticky blanket that traps bacteria and other foreign particles. If you look closely, you notice that this mucus blanket is actually moving.

The movement is due to the tiny hairs, which are called cilia. They beat very quickly, about six times a second, in a genetically predetermined direction designed to sweep the mucus and entrapped debris through the ostia and into the nose. Cilia normally are effective sweepers (see the sidebar "The Sweeping Cilia"). In fact, cilia are so efficient that they can overcome the downward pull of gravity. The ostia in the maxillary sinuses are close to the top of the sinus, so without the cilia sweeping mucus upward, the maxillary sinuses would never drain. Figure 2.4 shows the cilia.

FIGURE 2.4 Cilia

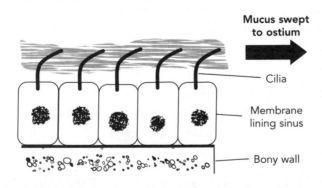

*This magnified view of the sinus lining shows microscopic hairlike structures (called cilia) on the membrane surface. The beating motion of these cilia sweeps a blanket of mucus that contains entrapped bacteria and debris out of the sinuses.*

## The Sweeping Cilia: A Sweet Demonstration

Just like the cilia inside your sinuses, you also have tiny hairs lining the inside of your nose to clear mucus. I sometimes demonstrate how cilia work by placing a crystal of saccharine inside a patient's nostril. Within a few minutes the saccharine is swept through the nasal cavity to the back of the throat, and the person tastes sweetness.

The continuous cycle of cilia-driven secretion of mucus is called mucociliary clearance, and it is essential for healthy sinus function. Because of mucociliary clearance, you are constantly swallowing small bits of mucus; if you're healthy, you usually don't even notice it. Healthy sinuses produce about eight ounces of mucus a day. That's quite a bit. It may be unpleasant to contemplate, but it's a necessary part of healthy sinus function.

When you're healthy and hydrated, mucus is thin and watery. When you're dehydrated, mucus gets thicker. The important thing is to get the right balance of mucus—not too little or too much, not too thick or too thin.

## Why We Have Sinuses: Seven Theories

In a sense, your sinuses do not even exist. After all, they are just empty spaces in your skull created by the intersection of bony walls surrounding your eyes. Think about it. No medical examiner conducting an autopsy could extract the sinuses from a human body and place them in a jar.

This idiosyncrasy has led anthropologists and physicians to ponder why humans developed sinuses in the first place. The truth is we don't really know. But there are at least seven theories:

1. **Sinuses lighten your load.** Having air pockets inside your skull makes your head weigh less than if it were solid bone and tissue. A lighter head may have made it easier for early

humans to evolve from walking on all fours to becoming a
two-legged, upright creature (see the sidebar "Neanderthal
Sinuses").

2. **Sinuses ease pressure.** Sinuses act as a safety valve of sorts
   when you experience dramatic changes in air pressure
   within the nasal cavity, such as during sneezing or nose
   blowing. Without sinuses, you might not be able to equalize
   pressure so well. Sneezing might be painful, and you might
   be more prone to breaking blood vessels, causing
   nosebleeds.

3. **Sinuses improve your ability to taste and smell.**
   Having an expanded surface area where odor molecules in
   the air can linger may help smell receptors in your nose do
   a better job. An enhanced sense of smell could have helped
   alert primitive humans to dangerous situations, such as
   smoke and fire or predators. And because an intact sense of
   smell is critical for perceiving flavor (just think how you
   lose smell and taste during a cold), sinuses could have
   allowed our ancestors to make smarter choices about which
   foods to eat and which to avoid.

4. **Sinuses protect your eyes and brain.** The sinuses serve
   as a trapdoor release mechanism inside your skull, easing
   the impact of blows to the head and thereby lessening
   potential damage to the eyes and brain. A recent illustration
   came during the 2000 baseball season, when Boston Red
   Sox pitcher Bryce Florie was hit in the eye by a line drive.
   Although the bones around his eyes fractured, Florie did
   not lose his sight. The thin bone of the roof of the
   maxillary sinus allowed pressure to be transmitted into the
   sinus instead of the eyeball. He returned to pitch the next
   season. From an evolutionary standpoint, you can see how
   this function might have benefited a caveman who
   encountered a club-wielding enemy.

5. **Sinuses help your voice.** As children learn from talking
   while pinching their noses, the human voice sounds
   different—and less pleasant—if you block the sinuses.

Having sinuses gives your voice tremendous resonance as well as a specific sound different from your neighbor's (call it a vocal signature). This enhanced vocal quality may have helped early humans communicate better as they gained the power of speech.

6. **Sinuses assist in air-conditioning.** As we've seen, the turbinates act as a treatment center for air as it passes through the nose on the way to the lungs. The mucus they produce filters unwanted particles, and their large surface area helps warm and moisturize cold, dry air. Because the sinuses provide a large additional supply of warm, moist mucous membranes, their role may be to enhance the air-conditioning process.

7. **Sinuses enable efficient facial growth.** The sinuses may play an important role in the development of our facial skeletons from birth through adolescence. The facial bones must grow in proper proportion to the skull as the brain and the cranial cavity enlarge. It's easy to imagine how the creation of hollow sinuses allows the body to expend less energy and fewer calories than it would to grow a facial skeleton of solid bone. The development of sinuses thus allows for more rapid and efficient facial growth.

It's likely that aspects of several of these theories combine to explain why we have sinuses. In my opinion, the final theory, on efficient facial growth, is one of the most plausible.

## Neanderthal Sinuses

Skull examinations reveal that the Neanderthal, who lived about three million years ago but eventually went extinct, had gigantic frontal sinuses. Our more direct ancestors, such as the Cro-Magnons, had smaller frontal sinuses. From an evolutionary standpoint, smaller frontal sinuses may have allowed more room for an enlarging brain.

## What's Next

We've now completed our tour of the Nasal House. With all the strange sights we've seen, you're probably relieved you live in a more conventional residence. But I hope you now have a solid understanding of where your sinuses are and how they work. So far I've mostly focused on what's happening when everything's working well. In the next chapter, we'll look at the many ways in which sinuses can malfunction.

CHAPTER 3

# When Healthy Sinuses Become Blocked

While sinus anatomy can be likened to a house, sinus function runs more like a car. With an automobile, you know there's a lot of firing and whirring going on under the hood, but as long as the car runs OK, you tend not to think about it. Then, after months or years without any problems, you start to hear a strange knocking sound. You hope it will go away, but instead the engine conks out on the highway, stranding you on your way to work.

Similarly, when your sinuses are healthy, you breathe in and out easily, and you never contemplate all the mucus production and air-conditioning occurring inside your nasal cavity. Then you notice you're congested, and after several days or weeks, you start to feel sinus pressure in your face or forehead. You hope it will go away, but instead you eventually find yourself so stuffed up or in so much pain you need to call your doctor.

I can't tell you how to keep your car on the road, but I can help you understand the chain of events that leads to sinusitis. In this chapter, we'll look at the causes of sinusitis and the resulting symptoms.

## The Direct Cause: It's the OMC

Although there are many root causes of sinusitis, they all fall into one of three broad categories: anatomical, genetic, and environmental (as shown in Table 3.1).

We'll cover each of these causes in subsequent chapters. For now, the critical fact is that regardless of the specific cause, in most cases, it will lead to a common triggering event: the ostiomeatal complex becomes obstructed.

Remember the OMC from Chapter 2? That's the "turnstile"—the narrow area in the middle meatus through which mucus drains from the sinuses into the nose. When the OMC gets blocked, in short order mucus backs up and the doors from the sinuses (the ostia) become blocked as well, as shown in Figure 3.1. The cilia stop beating effectively, and drainage from the sinuses stops or is severely curtailed.

That's when the real trouble begins. Glands within the sinuses continue to produce mucus, which cannot drain. Soon the blocked sinus fills up with mucus.

The warm, moist environment of the clogged sinus serves as what biologists refer to as the perfect culture medium. Even when you're healthy, small quantities of bacteria live in your nose and sinuses (see the sidebar "Bacteria in My Nose?"). But bacteria in the stagnant mucus rapidly multiply, so instead of a few hundred stray bacteria in your sinuses, you soon have several thousand, sev-

TABLE 3.1 Root Causes of Sinusitis

| Anatomical | Genetic | Environmental |
|---|---|---|
| Deviated septum | Cystic fibrosis | Air pollutants/chemicals |
| Nasal fracture | Immunodeficiency disorders | Allergies |
| Nasal polyps | Primary ciliary dyskinesia | Cigarette smoke |
| Scar tissue | Triad asthma | Colds |
| Tumors | | Dry indoor heating systems |
| | | Microorganisms (bacteria, fungi) |
| | | Sick building syndrome |

## FIGURE 3.1 OMC Blockage

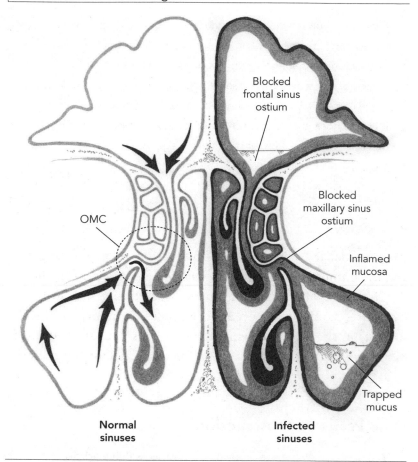

*Normal flow of mucus from inside the sinuses through the ostia and into the nasal cavity is shown on the left side of the diagram. Note that in the maxillary sinus, the mucus flows upward to reach the natural drainage ostium before turning downward to flow into the nose. The right side shows what happens when mucosa lining the sinuses becomes inflamed and blocks the OMC. Mucus trapped within the maxillary and frontal sinuses leads to bacterial overgrowth and sinusitis.*

eral hundred thousand, and eventually millions. Large numbers of bacteria constitute an infection.

Once your sinuses are infected, things quickly go from bad to worse. Your body kicks into action to fight the infection with what's known as the immune response. Unfortunately, this normally beneficial process is what ultimately makes you miserable.

## Bacteria in My Nose?

Even when you're healthy, bacteria live in your nose and sinuses. For example, the noses of an estimated 30 percent of the adult population are colonized with a particular bacteria called *Staphylococcus aureus*. This same bacteria can cause major illness if it makes its way into your lungs or beneath your skin, but having it in your nose and sinuses is not necessarily a problem, so long as mucus is draining. Without proper drainage, though, it can become a problem.

(As the sidebar "The Perils of Obstruction" explains, infection and the immune response can occur in many places in the body.)

To fight the bacteria, your mucus-secreting glands shift into overdrive, cranking out even more mucus than normal. Equally important, the mucous membrane that lines your sinus swells as blood vessels dilate in preparation for battle against the bacteria.

## The Perils of Obstruction

Although it may not seem obvious, the process that leads to sinusitis resembles what can happen almost anywhere in your body: obstruction leads to infection.

Think about it. Your body has numerous cavities that drain fluids regularly. Whether it's the urinary bladder, the ear, the large intestine, or a tiny sweat gland, if something blocks fluid from draining, the stage is set for bacteria to multiply and infection to develop. For example, when the bladder is blocked by a stone or an enlarged prostate, a urinary tract infection often results. An obstructed colon causes colitis, obstructed Eustachian tubes prompt an ear infection (otitis media), and a blocked skin gland produces acne.

FIGURE 3.2 The Sinusitis Cycle

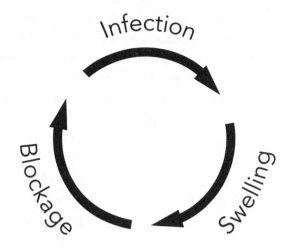

White blood cells in the blood circulating through this membrane are then recruited to attack, engulf, and destroy the bacteria. As this conflict rages, the white blood cells and the bacteria release a variety of substances that further stimulate the inflammatory process. These activators include interleukin, major basic protein, and leukotrienes.

The addition of white blood cells and bacteria to mucus makes it much thicker than usual, and often it becomes yellow or green (see the sidebar "Why Is Infected Mucus Green?"). This thick substance is referred to as pus or purulent mucus.

Some of the pus in the sinuses manages to squeeze out the ostia, through the OMC, and into the back of the nasal cavity. It tends to pool in the throat, causing irritation, or drain downward as troublesome postnasal drip.

A full-blown case of sinusitis is likely to worsen before it gets better. To fight the infection, the sinuses become more inflamed, which causes more swelling, which leads to more blockage, which allows for more bacterial overgrowth. You've now developed the "sinusitis cycle," as shown in Figure 3.2. This vicious cycle is eventually broken when the bacteria are eliminated by the body's

## Why Is Infected Mucus Green?

A surprising and little-known fact—that white blood cells are actually green—probably gives pus its greenish yellow hue. In fact, a mass of white blood cells is actually called a chloroma, which literally means "green tumor" in Greek. We call them white blood cells because under a microscope they appear whiter than the surrounding red blood cells. By-products from decaying bacteria are also thought to contribute to the discolored appearance of infected mucus.

There are many causes for increased white blood cells in your mucus, including allergy flare-ups and the common cold. So just because your clear mucus turns green doesn't mean you have sinusitis.

immune system, medications, or, occasionally, surgery. Then inflammation and blockage are finally reduced, enabling the sinuses to drain normally again.

## Sinusitis Symptoms: The Big Three

A number of symptoms can occur during a sinus infection. Let's start by looking at the Big Three that many people experience: pain and pressure, difficulty breathing and congestion, and post-nasal drip.

### Pain and Pressure

The dull, throbbing pain, ache, or pressure that is a hallmark of sinusitis results from inflamed tissue putting pressure on nerve endings in the lining of your sinuses. This pain's location is often specific to the infected sinus:

- Frontal sinusitis causes forehead pain or headache.
- Maxillary sinusitis causes cheek pain, which may radiate to the teeth in the upper jaw.

- Ethmoid sinusitis causes pain between the eyes or across the bridge of the nose.
- Sphenoid sinusitis causes pain behind the eyes, on the top of the scalp, or along the back of the head.

Depending on which part of the OMC is blocked, any one or all of your sinuses can become involved during an infection. If just one maxillary or frontal sinus is blocked, for instance, your symptoms may be localized to one cheek or one side of the head. If all four pairs of sinuses are infected (what's known as pansinusitis), your pain and pressure are usually more diffuse and may encompass the entire face or head.

## Difficulty Breathing and Congestion

The combination of swollen nasal membranes and excess mucus makes it difficult or impossible to breathe through your nose. This blockage can affect one or both sides of the nose. Because of the nasal cycle discussed in Chapter 2, it is not uncommon for nasal obstruction to alternate between sides.

For some sinus sufferers, the term *congestion* refers not to blocked nasal breathing but to a sense of fullness or blockage of the face, particularly in the cheeks. This sensation is caused by blockage of the sinuses themselves. When ostia swell shut, the mucous membranes in the sinuses absorb oxygen, creating negative pressure (or a vacuum), which can produce this sense of facial congestion or even pain.

## Postnasal Drip

As we've discussed, mucus from the sinuses normally drains in minute quantities into the nose and down the back of the throat before being swallowed. During an infection, increased secretion by the nose and sinuses results in a larger volume of mucus, which is often thick and yellow or green. This mucus, which may contain large quantities of bacteria and white blood cells, flows down the back of the nose and throat. Some people blow a large amount of mucus out the front of the nose as well.

31

## Other Sinusitis Symptoms

Along with the Big Three, other sinusitis symptoms can include any of the following:

- **Loss of smell.** The roof of the nasal cavity is lined with specialized tissue known as olfactory epithelium. This tissue contains specific smell receptors that are triggered by the odor molecules you breathe in. Swelling of the membranes in the nose can block these molecules from reaching the smell receptors, leaving you with a reduced sense of smell.
- **Loss of taste.** A normal sense of taste, particularly the ability to perceive different flavors, depends on an intact sense of smell. Consequently, many people who lose all or part of their sense of smell from sinusitis also describe a corresponding decrease in their sense of taste.
- **Bad breath.** The discolored mucus that drains from infected sinuses contains bacteria and debris that emit foul-smelling odors. As a result, thick mucus that runs down your throat may produce bad breath (halitosis) when these odors are exhaled. The bad breath you experience during sinusitis can be more powerful than conventional bad breath, which results from bacteria in the mouth. Mouthwash is likely to offer only a temporary reprieve.
- **Cough.** When mucus runs down the back of the throat, it may touch the vocal cords and trigger an involuntary cough response. Coughing is often worst upon awakening because mucus from the nose and sinuses pools in the throat overnight. If this mucus seeps between the vocal cords and into the trachea or windpipe, vigorous coughing may be needed to clear these secretions and protect the lungs.
- **Sore throat.** The thick mucus that drains during a sinus infection is more acidic than normal watery mucus, so it can irritate the membranes that line your throat.
- **Fatigue.** Your body uses extra energy to mount an immune response. This shifting of calorie reserves from

normal daily activity to infection fighting can leave you feeling tired. In addition, poor nasal breathing and frequent coughing during the night can cause poor quality sleep, resulting in less energy during the day.

- **Ear fullness.** Mucus drainage and inflammation from sinusitis may block the Eustachian tubes, passageways that connect your ears to the back of your nose (see Figure 2.2). When these tubes are open and function properly, they equalize pressure between the inside of the ears (known as the middle ear space) and the outside atmosphere. If they become blocked, you can develop an uncomfortable feeling of fullness or pressure in the ears, similar to what you may experience when you're on a plane descending from a high altitude.

- **Fever.** Occasionally, the body may mount a fever in response to the marked inflammation and the presence of a large quantity of bacteria during a sinus infection.

## What's Next

Just as a broken-down car forces you to visit an auto shop, malfunctioning nasal passages mean it's time to go to the doctor. Like a mechanic examining an engine, physicians can use their tools of the trade to pinpoint the problem and recommend treatment. In the next chapter, we'll look at what distinguishes sinusitis from related disorders and what you can expect when you visit your doctor.

# CHAPTER 4

# Making the Diagnosis: Do You Really Have Sinusitis?

Unless you have prior experience with sinusitis, you may have trouble distinguishing it from other ailments, such as colds and allergies. People often mistakenly confuse the three because so many of their symptoms are similar. But they are, in fact, different entities with different causes:

- **Colds.** Whereas sinusitis is caused by bacteria, colds are caused by viruses. These much smaller microorganisms invade the body's cells, where they reproduce and are eventually released into the bloodstream to invade other cells. The body's immune system is usually quite effective at controlling viral infections, so most colds go away within a week. Colds can occur at any time but are most common during winter (the cold season). What can be confusing is that it's not uncommon for a cold to precede a sinus infection.
- **Allergies.** Many of us have heard the old saying "If you sneeze more than three times, it's an allergy." Although not always correct, this does have some merit. Allergies are

usually caused by environmental irritants, such as pollen, dust mites, or pet dander, not bacteria or viruses. These irritants, known as allergens, activate an immune response that is different from the immune response to an infection. An antibody called immunoglobulin E (or IgE for short) triggers a specific type of white blood cell called a mast cell to release granules of histamine into the bloodstream. Histamine is a powerful molecule that causes the membranes of the upper respiratory tract, including the nose and sinuses, to swell and weep mucus. Histamine release can also trigger repeated sneezing and make your nose and eyes itch.

Allergies can be either perennial, meaning they occur year-round, or seasonal. Allergies to dust and pet dander are often perennial. Seasonal allergies tend to be worst during the spring, when flowers and trees bloom, and the fall, when ragweed is in the air. As with colds, allergies may precede and trigger sinusitis.

Table 4.1 lists many of the differences between sinusitis, colds, and allergies. Understanding these differences is helpful, but it

TABLE 4.1 Comparing Sinusitis, Cold, and Allergy Symptoms

| Symptom | Sinusitis | Cold | Allergy |
|---|---|---|---|
| Facial pressure/pain | Yes | Sometimes | Sometimes |
| Duration of illness | More than 10 days | Less than 10 days | Varies |
| Nasal discharge | Thick, yellow-green | Thick and whitish or thin and watery | Clear, thin, watery |
| Itchy eyes | No | No | Yes |
| Headache | Yes | Sometimes | Sometimes |
| Bad breath | Sometimes | No | No |
| Cough | Sometimes | Yes | Sometimes |
| Nasal congestion | Yes | Yes | Sometimes |
| Sneezing | No | Yes | Yes |
| Fatigue/weakness | Sometimes | Yes | Sometimes |
| Sore throat | Sometimes | Yes | Sometimes |

won't make your symptoms go away. If severe nasal symptoms linger for more than a week, it's advisable to see your doctor.

## Primary Care Visit

Your primary care physician will begin by asking you to describe your current symptoms and how long you've had them. In addition to the Big Three—pain and pressure, difficulty breathing and congestion, and postnasal drip—she will probably inquire about other symptoms, such as loss of smell, sore throat, cough, and fatigue. She will also ask about your history: Have similar symptoms occurred in the past? How often? What medications have you tried? Do you have allergies? Do you smoke? What are your home and work environments like?

Try to be prepared to answer these questions as thoroughly as possible. A good patient history is the single most important tool your doctor has to confirm the diagnosis of sinusitis. This same history is also critical for determining whether something other than sinusitis could be causing your problems. For example, if you only have facial pain without congestion or drainage, your problem could be neurological in nature, with migraine headaches and neuralgia as possibilities, and you may be referred to a neurologist. And if you are sneezing and have itchy eyes and your postnasal drip remains thin and watery, it's likely you have allergies, and you may be referred to an allergist.

Once the history is completed, your primary care physician may look inside your nose with a small flashlight. She won't be able to see into your sinuses, but she can see the front portion of the inferior turbinates and assess how much swelling there is and whether any pus is present.

Some doctors may also tap on your forehead or cheeks—a technique known as percussion of the sinuses—and ask you if it hurts. Although there's no harm from tapping, you should be aware that it's not a reliable indicator of sinusitis. Many patients who have sinusitis have no sinus tenderness during an infection, while others with completely normal sinuses will complain of pain when their forehead or cheeks are tapped.

## CT Scan

While a careful patient history with a nasal examination is often enough to determine whether you have sinusitis, your doctor may also order a computed tomography (CT) scan to confirm the diagnosis. A CT scan is a radiological technique that has largely replaced plain sinus x-rays for evaluating sinus disease. A CT scan is a series of x-ray pictures, each a thin slice ranging from one to three millimeters in thickness, that combine to form a three-dimensional view. It allows your doctor to view the interior of your nose and sinuses in exquisite detail.

A CT scan of the sinuses is painless and takes less than five minutes. You lie down on a table that slides through a large doughnut-shaped scanner. With newer models, you can see above and below this device, so claustrophobia is not a problem.

There are two kinds of sinus CT scans: limited and full. A limited scan typically shows four or five vertical slices, with at least one cut through each of the sinuses to identify any polyps, cysts, or entrapped fluid. A full scan usually involves more than twenty vertical and horizontal slices. The larger number of slices enables your doctor to see the individual sinus ostia, including the OMC, and whether or not they're blocked. A limited scan is less expensive than a full scan; in general, primary care doctors order limited scans, and ear, nose, and throat (ENT) specialists order full scans.

Either way, results are usually available within minutes and may be viewed on printed films or a computer screen. On a CT scan, air shows up black and bone appears white, as shown in Figure 4.1. Gray areas in the sinuses often signify abnormalities, such as pus, mucus, polyps, or cysts. When looking at sinus CT scans, you should keep in mind the general rule of thumb that black is good and gray is bad, with cysts being one exception (see the sidebar "Why Sinus Cysts Are No Problem").

**FIGURE 4.1** CT Scan of Clear and Blocked Sinuses

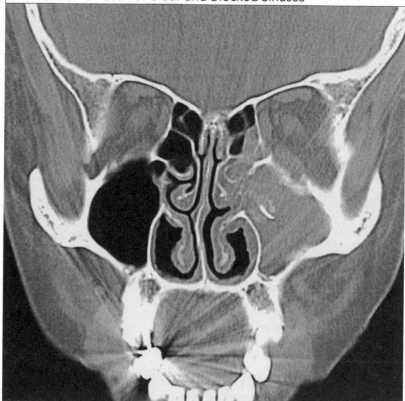

*This sinus CT scan shows normal air-filled sinuses, which are black in appearance, on the left side. On the right side, obstructed maxillary and ethmoid sinuses are shown; they appear gray because they are filled with fluid.*

## Treatment and Referral

If your doctor concludes that you have sinusitis, in most cases she will prescribe an antibiotic and advise you to take an over-the-counter decongestant. If she believes allergies are playing a role, she may also prescribe a nasal steroid spray and recommend an antihistamine. I'll discuss these and other medications in detail in Chapters 9, 10, and 11.

A course of antibiotics will often eliminate the infection or at least reduce it to the point that your symptoms recede. But if the

## Why Sinus Cysts Are No Problem

It's common for CT scans to reveal cysts (mucus-filled sacs about the size of a grape) inside sinuses. Patients are often concerned about this discovery and wonder if immediate treatment is needed.

It isn't. Although cysts in other parts of the body (such as the neck, ovaries, or kidneys) can cause problems, they're almost always harmless in the nasal cavity. Here, a cyst develops when a mucus-secreting gland becomes blocked, perhaps by a localized inflammation or for no apparent reason. Cysts are especially common in the maxillary sinuses.

Cysts usually rupture painlessly when they reach a certain size; the mucus then drains out of the sinuses and into the nasal cavity. People are usually oblivious to this event, although they might notice a salty taste. In rare instances in which a cyst causes pain or becomes large enough to block a sinus and prompt infection, it may be necessary to remove it surgically.

sinus blockage remains, the infection may return a short time later. If you have more than three sinus infections in a year, your primary care doctor may refer you to an ENT specialist, also known as an otolaryngologist (see the sidebar "It's Greek to Me").

It's not difficult to find a qualified ENT specialist. Most primary care doctors have a group of ENT specialists they regularly refer patients to. As a general rule, if you're comfortable with your primary care physician, you should have confidence she will refer you to a capable ENT specialist. You might also ask your friends for recommendations. The point to be made here is that any ENT specialist certified by the American Board of Otolaryngology (see aboto.org) has the training and expertise to treat sinusitis.

## Off to the ENT Doctor

Like a primary care physician, an ENT doctor will begin by asking you about your history of sinusitis. This history may go into

## It's Greek to Me

Although it's quite a mouthful, the formal name for an ear, nose, and throat specialist is otolaryngologist, derived from Greek. *Oto* means "ear," and *larynx* refers to the voice box or throat. The name used to be even longer—otorhinolaryngologist—but the *rhino* (meaning "nose") was dropped in an attempt to make the term more manageable. Although otolaryngology is still the formal department name in most medical schools, most physicians in this specialty refer to themselves as ENT doctors.

greater detail, especially if it's your first encounter with this doctor.

Next, he will likely examine your nose, using a nasal speculum to gently spread your nostrils and look inside. If he wishes to get a closer view, he'll use an endoscope, a thin, high-resolution telescope with a light on one end and an eyepiece on the other. Figure 4.2 shows an endoscopic examination.

Nasal endoscopy is mildly invasive, so he'll first spray your nasal passages with a topical decongestant (which enlarges the nasal passages by temporarily reducing swelling in your mucous membranes) and a mild topical anesthetic (which reduces the tickle sensation and prevents you from sneezing). These medications help ensure that endoscopy is not painful, although some people may still find it mildly uncomfortable.

Endoscopy gives your ENT doctor a detailed view of what's going on in your nasal cavity. He can see four important things:

- if the mucous membranes are inflamed
- if the middle meatus is draining pus
- if the turbinates are enlarged
- if polyps are blocking the sinuses

Polyps are small growths ranging in size from a pea to a grape that are attached by tiny stalks to the sinus walls, as shown in Fig-

41

**FIGURE 4.2** Endoscopic Exam

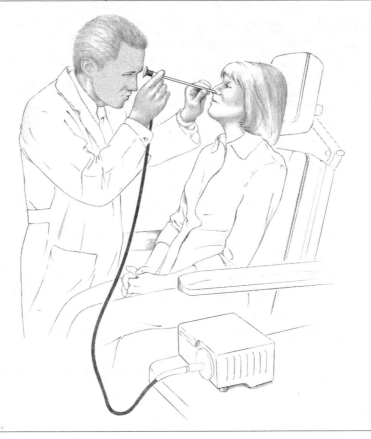

*During a nasal endoscopic examination, the doctor looks into the nose with a thin endoscope attached by a fiber-optic cable to a light source.*

ure 4.3. Although the precise cause of polyps is unknown, they tend to occur in individuals whose sinus mucosa is chronically inflamed (see the sidebar "Are Sinus Polyps like Polyps Elsewhere in the Body?").

As polyps continue to grow, they eventually block the nasal airway, causing congestion, difficulty breathing through the nose, and an impaired sense of smell. When polyps become large enough, they block the sinus drainage passages, leading to overgrowth of bacteria and the resultant pain of a sinus infection.

**FIGURE 4.3** Polyps

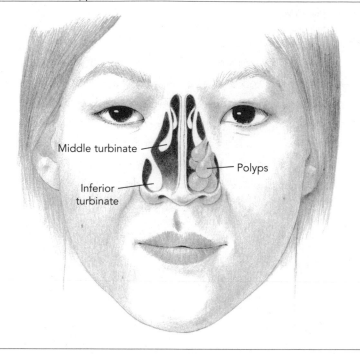

Middle turbinate

Polyps

Inferior turbinate

*Chronic inflammation leads to growth of polyps that can block the nasal and sinus cavities.*

In addition to polyps, another common finding during endoscopic examination is enlarged turbinates. The inferior turbinates, in particular, can become large and swollen from what's known as allergic rhinitis (literally, "inflamed nose"). Unlike sinusitis, this form of environmental allergy causes swelling of the nasal passages but leaves the sinuses unaffected.

People with allergic rhinitis have many of the same allergy symptoms as those listed in Table 4.1, but their CT scan shows clear sinuses. Allergy medications will usually provide relief. If not, your doctor may want to refer you for allergy testing (as discussed in the next section).

Endoscopy does not enable an ENT specialist to view inside your sinuses because the ostia are too small for the endoscope to

## Are Sinus Polyps like Polyps Elsewhere in the Body?

No. Unlike polyps of the colon and bladder, which can be cancerous, sinus polyps are almost never malignant. Furthermore, having sinus polyps does not increase your chances of having polyps elsewhere in the body (and vice versa). The reason for this difference is that nasal polyps arise from a unique embryologic layer of tissue (known as the Schneiderian membrane) that lines the nose and sinuses and is found nowhere else in the body.

enter. To learn what's going on inside the sinuses, your ENT doctor will probably obtain a sinus CT scan, if you haven't already had one.

## Other Tests

In almost all cases, a detailed patient history, nasal endoscopy, and a CT scan will provide your ENT doctor with all the information he needs to make an accurate diagnosis. Occasionally, though, additional tests are ordered. As the sidebar "Do I Need an MRI?" explains, an MRI is usually not one of them.

- **Allergy tests.** If environmental allergies appear to be the underlying cause of your sinusitis, you may be a candidate for allergy testing. Skin tests entail exposing your skin to a large variety of allergens (substances that trigger allergies) by either pinprick or needle injection. An alternative to skin testing is a radioallergosorbent test (RAST), a blood test that measures amounts of an antibody (IgE) your body produces to fight allergies. Both skin tests and RASTs are commonly performed by allergists and otolaryngologists with expertise in allergies.
- **Cultures.** If endoscopy shows pus, an ENT specialist may obtain a culture with a small Q-tip to determine which

## Do I Need an MRI?

Patients sometimes ask if they would benefit from an MRI (magnetic resonance imaging) to evaluate their sinuses. The answer is usually no. Unlike CT scans, MRIs do not show bone, so details about the bony walls and anatomy of the sinuses shown on CT are not visible with MRI. Even the OMC is not easily seen. MRIs are excellent for delineating soft tissue, so they can be useful in the rare case of a suspected sinus tumor.

bacteria are present and how sensitive they are to various antibiotics. These endoscopically guided cultures may be particularly helpful for patients who have not responded as expected to antibiotics.

A second type of culture—those performed by placing a large Q-tip in the nostril (also called a nasal swab)—can be problematic because it's hard to distinguish between bacteria that are harmful and cause sinus infections and bacteria that harmlessly live in the nose.

- **Blood tests.** Your physician may order general blood tests if he suspects you have a systemic (whole-body) illness that's triggering your sinusitis.

## What's Next

Depending on the duration of your symptoms, you may be diagnosed with either acute or chronic sinusitis. The causes and treatment options for these two types can be very different. In the next chapter, we'll take a look at acute sinusitis.

# CHAPTER 5

# Acute Sinusitis: When a Bad Cold Gets Worse

When you get a sinus infection, one of two things happens: you get better or you don't. If your symptoms are gone within a month, or even two or three, you had acute sinusitis. But if the pain, congestion, drainage, or other symptoms last longer than three months, you have chronic sinusitis.

What's so magical about the three-month time period? Nothing. It's just an arbitrary cutoff that experts in the field have agreed to. If a health problem persists for longer than three months, it seems reasonable to label it as chronic.

This time frame, not the cause or symptoms, is the main thing that distinguishes acute sinusitis from chronic sinusitis. The mechanics of the infection and the way you feel when you're sick are essentially the same for both. Aside from the duration, about the only significant difference is that people with acute sinusitis are more likely to run a fever.

In practical terms, however, there is a real difference. People who have acute sinusitis tend not to think of themselves as having a serious problem. They have an episode of sinusitis, which slows them down for a few days or weeks, but then it goes away, and they get on with their lives. People with chronic sinusitis, on the other hand, are engaged in an ongoing struggle. Their sinusitis symptoms persist or keep returning, which can have a major impact on their overall health and quality of life.

## How a Common Cold Can Lead to Sinusitis

We have a good understanding of what causes acute sinusitis and how to treat it. Most cases are preceded by a bad cold, also known as an upper respiratory infection, or URI for short. Such colds are caused by viruses. Although there are dozens of cold-causing viruses, rhinovirus (literally, "nose virus") is a common culprit.

Most of the time, the common cold goes away without medical treatment, and no further problems ensue. But in a small percentage of cases—less than 5 percent—the cold transitions to acute sinusitis. This progression is most likely to occur in people who have narrow or blocked sinus ostia, a condition that predisposes them to sinusitis.

Why? Sinus drainage is often impaired during a cold because of swelling that occurs in the nasal cavity. When people with narrow ostia get a cold, their partially blocked sinuses may shut down completely, trapping mucus in the sinus. This scenario enables bacteria in the sinuses to multiply, causing an infection.

Acute sinusitis is usually caused by one of three bacteria: *Streptococcus pneumoniae* (also called pneumococcus), *Haemophilus influenzae* (H flu), and *Moraxella catarrhalis* (M cat). As I described in Chapter 3, the infection sets off a chain of events that causes a constellation of symptoms, including facial pressure or headache, nasal drainage, and congestion.

By the time you develop acute sinusitis, the virus that caused the initial cold is usually no longer present (not that this makes you feel any better). Instead, you now have what's known as a secondary infection, meaning an infection that's bacterial rather than viral.

This secondary infection is likely to be more persistent than the initial infection, due to the vicious cycle of sinusitis. The bacteria cause swelling, which prevents the ostia from draining properly, which leads to more bacterial growth, which causes more swelling—and the cycle repeats.

Despite bacteria's propensity for reproducing, in most cases the body's immune system successfully overcomes the infection, and sinusitis recedes before you go to a doctor or take medication. But if you notice no improvement after seven to ten days of having sinusitis, a call or visit to the doctor is advisable.

## Easing Symptoms

Acute sinusitis will make you feel lousy for several days. Here are some things you can do to ease the discomfort while the infection runs its course:

- **Pick a painkiller.** An analgesic relieves pain from sinus pressure and headache. I tell patients to take whichever pain reliever they're accustomed to using: acetaminophen (Tylenol), ibuprofen (Advil, Motrin), or aspirin can all help.
- **Don't dry out.** Avoid dehydration by drinking at least three extra glasses of water a day. This additional fluid intake thins the mucus trapped in your sinuses, enabling it to drain more easily.
- **Irrigate your nose.** Rinsing your nasal passages with salt water, a practice known as nasal irrigation, can help drain infected mucus. I'll discuss this technique in detail in Chapter 7. If you're in the midst of a bout with acute sinusitis, feel free to jump ahead to that section.
- **Seek steam.** Keeping your nasal passages moist also aids drainage. You can do this by carefully holding your face over a pot of boiling water and inhaling the steam. The steam from a bowl of chicken soup or hot tea may be beneficial. And a long, steamy shower can also help.
- **Use ice.** Putting ice on the affected sinus may relieve pain. You can use an ice mask from a drugstore, a cold compress, or a bag of ice.

## Medications for Acute Sinusitis

If you do go to the doctor with acute sinusitis, there's a good chance you'll end up taking two types of medicines: antibiotics and decongestants. If your doctor recommends only one medicine, it's most likely to be an antibiotic.

### Antibiotics

Penicillin and amoxicillin were once effective antibiotics for the treatment of sinusitis. During the past thirty years, however, many bacteria have developed resistance to these antibiotics. Although amoxicillin is still commonly prescribed as a first-line antibiotic for patients with acute sinusitis, it fails to clear the infection in up to 30 percent of cases. Many doctors now prescribe Augmentin, which contains amoxicillin and another medication, clavulanate. The addition of clavulanate ensures elimination of resistant strains of H flu and M cat. A doctor may choose a different antibiotic for patients who are allergic to amoxicillin, such as azithromycin (Zithromax), clarithromycin (Biaxin), or telithromycin (Ketek).

Although most antibiotics are prescribed for ten days, azithromycin comes in both three-day (Tri-Pak) and five-day (Z-Pak) preparations; these are adequate for many cases of acute sinusitis. Other commonly prescribed antibiotics include cefpodoxime (Vantin) and cefdinir (Omnicef). I'll discuss these and other antibiotics in more detail in Chapter 11.

### Decongestants

Decongestants are available over the counter in two forms: nasal sprays (such as Afrin, Dristan, and Neo-Synephrine) and pills (such as Sudafed). They act by shrinking the swollen mucous membranes that line the nose and sinuses, particularly around the engorged turbinates and blocked ostia. Ideally, a decongestant enables you to breathe better during an infection and hastens the end of your sickness by opening your ostia long enough to allow the infected mucus to drain.

*Spray Decongestants.* The advantage of sprays is that they offer near-instant relief. This is because their active ingredient (oxymetazoline or phenylephrine) is applied in high concentration directly to the affected area. However, sprays carry a major draw-back, what's known as rebound. If they're used too long, once the medication wears off, the swelling returns—and now it's even worse than when you started using the spray. For this reason, such nasal sprays should be used for no more than two or three days and only for acute infections, not chronic.

If rebound does develop, it can be very difficult to stop using nasal sprays. People can become dependent on them, needing a spray every few hours just to breathe through their noses, even during the night. They may carry a bottle of nasal spray with them 24-7 and have extra bottles in their glove compartment, medicine cabinet, and nightstand. I've treated many patients who became hooked on these sprays for years, long after the initial infection for which they originally took the medication had left their body.

One way to reduce the risk of dependence is to use a shorter-acting or milder spray. For instance, Neo-Synephrine, which is available in a mild-strength four-hour dose, is less likely to cause rebound than Afrin, which is only available in the longer-acting twelve-hour formula.

If you or someone you know does become dependent on nasal sprays, breaking the habit isn't easy, but it can be done. Some people go cold turkey. It may mean one or two sleepless nights, but after forty-eight hours, they're breathing through their nose again without the need for sprays. If attempts to stop on your own fail, a doctor can prescribe a combination of steroid pills and nasal steroid sprays during the withdrawal period. This combo blunts the rebound effect and can make recovery quite a bit easier.

It's worth noting that rebound is not just an issue for people with acute sinusitis. Anyone with blocked nasal breathing, including people who just have a bad cold, can get hooked on nasal sprays. The bottom line is that they can help you get through the

THE SINUSES IN HEALTH AND DISEASE

most difficult spell during a bout of nasal congestion, but you should stop using them after two or three days.

*Oral Decongestants.* The active ingredient in oral decongestants is pseudoephedrine, which shrinks swollen mucous membranes. Because oral decongestants are not applied directly to the affected area, they are slower acting than sprays and do not provide the same immediate relief. They can nonetheless be effective, draining infected mucus and enabling you to breathe more easily. Furthermore, you can take them for long periods without the risk of rebound.

But oral decongestants also have drawbacks. The medication in pills circulates through your entire body, so you may experience certain side effects. Oral decongestants cause rapid heartbeat or palpitations in some people and are not recommended for those with hypertension. They also can make you feel jittery and cause insomnia. If that's the case, it's best to avoid taking them at night.

## My Choice of Medications for Acute Sinusitis

When I see patients with their first episode of acute sinusitis, if their symptoms are relatively mild, I'll usually prescribe a ten-day course of the antibiotic amoxicillin (250 mg three times a day). If there's not significant improvement in their discomfort within three to five days, I may switch them to Augmentin (500 mg twice a day for ten days), which will cover most resistant organisms. If symptoms are severe at the outset or they've already been treated with a first-line antibiotic like amoxicillin and their symptoms returned, I'll prescribe Augmentin.

A five-day course of Zithromax (Z-Pak) or Ketek (Ketek Pak) is also very effective for acute sinusitis, but they're more expensive. I usually reserve these antibiotics, as well as Biaxin, for patients who cannot take amoxicillin or Augmentin because of a penicillin allergy.

If facial pain or pressure is the main problem and the patient has little or no associated congestion, I'll only prescribe an antibiotic. If, however, the patient is having difficulty breathing through the nose, I'll add a decongestant to the mix. For moderate congestion, I recommend over-the-counter Sudafed (a 30-mg pill three or four times a day) or an over-the-counter sinus medication that contains pseudoephedrine as one of its active ingredients. For congestion so severe that a person has difficulty functioning during the day or sleeping at night, I'll also recommend a decongestant spray, such as the four-hour dose of Neo-Synephrine (three times a day for two or three days).

## Surgery for Acute Sinusitis?

Surgery is almost never used to treat acute sinusitis. However, in rare cases it may be necessary, particularly if the bacterial infection breaks through one of the bony sinus walls. The most common site for this complication to occur is at the very thin bone that separates the ethmoid sinus and the eye socket. This bony portion is known as the lamina papyracea (literally, "paper plate" in Latin). An abscess forms near the eye and can lead to vision loss unless it is drained.

## What's Next

An episode of acute sinusitis can be painful and frustrating. But in most cases, it eventually goes away either with or without the aid of a physician. If the infection does not subside or keeps returning, then you may have chronic sinusitis, the subject of the remainder of this book. In the next chapter, I'll explain how chronic sinusitis is actually many different diseases—what I call the Sinusitis Spectrum—and help you develop a treatment plan that's right for you.

CHAPTER

# The Sinusitis Spectrum: Where Do You Fit In?

As you've seen, sinusitis can be either acute or chronic. That's pretty simple. But what if I told you that chronic sinusitis is actually not one but five or ten or even twenty-five different diseases? It complicates matters, but it's true.

While modern medicine has a long way to go before we understand chronic sinusitis as well as we do acute sinusitis, it's increasingly clear that chronic sinusitis is a spectrum of diseases. I like to use the term *Sinusitis Spectrum* to explain why patients with chronic sinusitis respond so differently to treatment. A medication that benefits one person may have little or no effect on another. And the same surgery that permanently cures one person may need to be repeated a few years later on another. Figuring out where you fit on the Sinusitis Spectrum can help you put your own case into perspective. Once you've done that, you can focus on the treatments most likely to benefit you.

## Three General Types: Locals, Systemics, and Intermediates

For simplicity's sake, the Sinusitis Spectrum breaks down into three general categories (see Figure 6.1). On one end of the spec-

FIGURE 6.1 The Sinusitis Spectrum

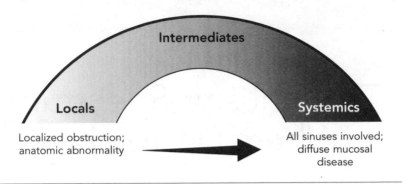

*Everyone with sinusitis can be found somewhere along the Sinusitis Spectrum, based on the cause and severity of his or her disease. The spectrum is divided into three main groups—Locals, Intermediates, and Systemics—with each group responding to the various treatments for sinusitis in different ways.*

trum are people whose sinusitis stems from physical abnormalities within their nasal cavity or sinuses. People in this group have a site-specific, localized problem, so let's call them Locals.

On the opposite end of the spectrum are those whose sinusitis can be traced to a more general disorder affecting other areas of their bodies, not just their nose and sinuses. You might think of your body as a large system, so we'll call them Systemics.

In between these two extremes lies a group whose problem is more difficult to pin down. They may have both problems—physical abnormalities within their nasal cavity and malfunctions affecting their entire bodies—or they may have neither. Often, the source of their problem cannot be easily traced. Conceptually, people in this group fall in between Locals and Systemics, so let's call them Intermediates.

Now let's examine these groups in more depth and also look at which treatments are most likely to benefit each group.

## Locals

Locals have a straightforward anatomical problem. Examples include people whose sinusitis can be traced to any of the following:

- a localized OMC obstruction
- a deviated septum
- an enlarged middle turbinate (also known as a concha bullosa)
- dental problems, such as an infected tooth root that spreads to the maxillary sinus

*Signs and Symptoms.* You may be in this group if:

- you have symptoms on one side of the face or head and not the other
- your postnasal drip and other symptoms completely clear between sinus infections
- you have no history of allergies or have had negative allergy tests

*Treatment.* Medication can be effective treatment for Locals, but the symptoms often return once medication is stopped (see Figure 6.2). That's because medicine does not address the underlying anatomical problem that caused the infection.

If medications don't work, or if you do not wish to take them indefinitely, surgery to correct the anatomical problem is often effective. Such treatment might include a procedure known as a septoplasty to straighten the deviated septum, extraction of an infected tooth, or sinus surgery to clear an obstruction of the OMC. Locals are more likely than those with other forms of sinusitis to be cured by surgery; for this reason, it's often recommended early in the treatment course if nasal endoscopy or CT scans reveal an anatomical defect.

## Systemics

Like an engine that idles too fast or too slow, the airway system among Systemics is off kilter. Some stimulus, usually unknown, causes chronic inflammation of the mucous membranes lining the nose and sinuses. This chronic inflammation often affects the lining of the lungs as well, which is why so many Systemics also have

57

**FIGURE 6.2** Symptom Patterns of Sinusitis

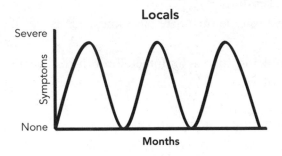

## Locals

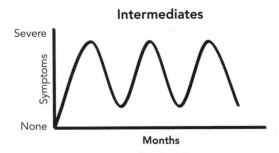

## Intermediates

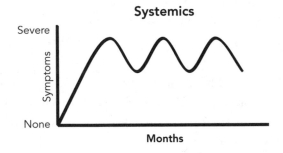

## Systemics

*These graphs show the common patterns of chronic sinusitis. Locals have complete clearing of symptoms between infections. Intermediates improve between infections but often have some residual symptoms, like postnasal drip or congestion. Systemics have chronic symptoms that fluctuate but never seem to go away.*

asthma (up to 30 percent). Viewed under a microscope, inflammation of the mucous membranes in the lungs is so similar to that of the nose and sinuses that Systemics may have what can be referred to as one airway disease. In other words, the underlying process that causes their sinusitis is also causing their asthma.

There is a major difference, however, between the way the mucous membranes of the sinuses and the lungs react to chronic inflammation. For unknown reasons, inflammation in the sinuses leads to the formation of polyps. These grapelike growths, which arise from the inflamed lining of the nose and sinuses, can be quite large in Systemics, causing significant congestion.

Examples of Systemics include people with any of the following:

- CT scans showing blockage or membrane swelling in all sinuses
- polyps on both sides of the nose
- triad asthma, a condition in which patients have asthma, nasal polyps, and an allergy to aspirin

**Signs and Symptoms.** You may be in this group if:

- you have congestion and pressure on both sides of your face
- you have difficulty breathing through both sides of your nose
- your postnasal drip is thick, yellow or green mucus, and it never seems to go away
- you have lost your sense of smell
- you have severe allergies

**Treatment.** Systemics are the most difficult group to treat. Surgery to remove polyps and other obstructions may offer temporary relief but often needs to be repeated when the obstruction recurs. Medications such as oral steroids often help, but they may cause intolerable side effects. In many cases, the challenge is finding a regimen that can be followed in the long term without causing unwelcome side effects.

## Intermediates
Intermediates are people who do not fit neatly into either of the two other groups. Examples of Intermediates include people with any of the following:

- CT scans showing involvement of sinuses on both sides of the face, but not all of the sinuses
- allergies severe enough to have required allergy shots at some time in their lives
- allergies in combination with an anatomical obstruction, such as a deviated septum or an enlarged middle turbinate (concha bullosa)
- frequent flare-ups of symptoms during allergy season or in the workplace, suggesting an environmental trigger

**Signs and Symptoms.** You may be in this group if:

- your nasal obstruction and symptoms alternate from one side of the face to the other
- you have intermittent postnasal drip that becomes thick and discolored during infections
- your symptoms get better but don't always clear completely between sinus infections

**Treatment.** Treatment for Intermediates varies depending on where you fit along the Sinusitis Spectrum—in other words, whether you're closer to Locals or Systemics. Often, numerous treatment approaches are tried before finding one that is moderately successful. Surgery typically offers mixed results; in most patients, it reduces the frequency and severity of sinus infections but does not provide a full cure.

Don't worry if you don't match all the traits for one of the three categories; very few people do. View Table 6.1 as a guideline to help you get an idea of your place in the Sinusitis Spectrum. If you're still uncertain, your doctor may be able to provide guidance.

## A Treatment Plan That's Right for You

Decades from now, I expect that most patients with chronic sinusitis will be able to undergo a simple blood test and genetic

**TABLE 6.1** Symptoms and Treatments Across the Sinusitis Spectrum

| | Locals | Intermediates | Systemics |
|---|---|---|---|
| **Symptom** | **Symptom's Presence, Severity, and/or Frequency** | | |
| Nasal obstruction | On one side only | Alternating from side to side | On both sides |
| Facial pain/ headache | On one side or both | On both sides; moderate to severe pain | On both sides; mild to severe pain |
| Postnasal drainage | Only during infections | Usually present; worse during infections | Constant |
| Environmental allergies | None or mild | Often have allergies | Often have allergies |
| Aspirin allergy | No | No | Yes, if triad asthma |
| Asthma | No | Sometimes | Often |
| Impaired sense of smell | No | No or mild | Often, sometimes severely |
| Polyps | None or small; localized | Intermediate size; involving mainly ethmoid region | Large, diffuse; involving all sinuses |
| **CT Scan** | **Location of Disease** | | |
| | On one side or limited disease on both sides | On both sides, but not all sinuses | All sinuses |
| **Treatment** | **Is This Treatment Likely to Prove Beneficial?** | | |
| Nasal irrigation | Yes | Yes | Yes |
| Use of indoor humidifier during winter months | No | Yes | Yes |
| Nonantibiotic sinus medications (decongestants, antihistamines, mucus-thinning agents) | May provide partial relief | May provide marked relief, especially if allergies present | May provide partial relief |
| Nasal steroid sprays | No | Yes, especially if allergies present | Yes |
| Antibiotics | Yes, but infection may recur months later | Yes, but infection may return weeks later | Yes, but infection often recurs immediately after stopping |
| Oral steroids | No | May benefit | Yes |
| Surgery | Often effective | Usually effective, but not curative | Sometimes effective, but often needs to be repeated |

analysis to determine the precise type of sinusitis they have. Then we'll be able to use gene therapy to replace a missing enzyme or add a strand of deleted DNA, eliminating the inflammatory process that serves as the root cause of most cases of sinusitis.

But for now, we know very little about the underlying causes of chronic sinusitis. We tend to lump all sinusitis patients together and treat them with the same regimens, even though they have many different diseases.

Until we understand the answers to fundamental questions about the underlying causes of sinusitis, the best thing you can do to control your symptoms is develop a treatment plan based on where you fit on the Sinusitis Spectrum. Some of these treatments can be self-administered. Others need to be done in cooperation with your doctor.

## What's Next

In the next chapter, we'll explore one of the simplest and most effective treatments for sinusitis: nasal irrigation.

# Nonsurgical Treatments for Sinusitis

# CHAPTER 7

# Nasal Irrigation: A Key to Healthier Sinuses

If your mother sent you off to school as a child with the admonition to "keep your nose clean," she was unwittingly giving you sage advice that can help in your struggle with sinusitis. Keeping your nose clean—through a practice known as nasal irrigation—can be a key to reducing sinusitis symptoms.

Nasal irrigation (also known as nasal lavage or nasal rinsing) is easy and inexpensive and has no negative side effects. I strongly advise people who suffer from nasal congestion and drainage to incorporate it into their daily hygiene routine. A popular option is to brush and flush; in other words, irrigate twice a day, right after brushing your teeth.

Nasal irrigation washes out excess mucus that might otherwise lead to bothersome drainage or blocked breathing. Along with the mucus, you're also flushing out unwanted debris (including bacteria, mold, dust, and other irritants) that can cause nasal tissues to swell. So nasal irrigation really achieves two goals: it opens more room to breathe and clears obstructions that might predispose you to sinusitis (see the sidebar "Researchers Agree: Irrigation Really Works").

## Researchers Agree: Irrigation Really Works

If you're the type who demands scientific evidence before you start squirting things up your nose, you'll be happy to hear that a small but growing body of evidence demonstrates nasal irrigation really does work.

Eight randomized, controlled studies have assessed nasal irrigation. All eight "reported significant positive outcomes on a variety of measures," according to a February 2004 letter to the *Journal of Family Practice* by Dr. David Rabago of the University of Wisconsin. Dr. Rabago's own study found that patients with histories of frequent acute or chronic sinusitis who used nasal irrigation for six months reported improved quality of life, improved nasal symptoms, and reduced use of nasal sprays and antibiotics.

## Keeping It Simple: Using a Bulb Syringe

There are many tools for irrigating your nose, but I'm a fan of the KISS (keep it simple, stupid) principle. All you really need is a bulb syringe—a common device used to clean newborn infants' noses that looks like a cross between a lightbulb and a turkey baster (see Figure 7.1). A bulb syringe costs under $5; some drugstores and most medical supply stores carry them. A small ear syringe, used to flush wax from the ear canal, also works, but I prefer the nasal version because its larger size allows for more efficient irrigation, and the tapered tip fits comfortably in the nostril.

While standing in front of your bathroom or kitchen sink, follow these steps:

1. Fill an eight-ounce glass with lukewarm tap water.
2. Stir in approximately one teaspoon of table salt. The exact amount is not critical; just make it slightly salty to taste.
3. Fill the bulb with the saltwater solution.
4. Lean over the sink, and with your head bowed slightly, insert the tip of the syringe just inside your nostril.

**FIGURE 7.1** Nasal Irrigation with a Bulb Syringe

*Nasal irrigation is performed by leaning over a sink and flushing each nostril with salt water.*

5. Gently squeeze the bulb. The solution will run up into your nose and then drain back out the nostril into the sink. Sometimes the water may run to the back of the nose and drain out the opposite nostril—that's not a problem. It's also OK if some of the water drains into the back of your mouth—just spit it out.

6. Refill the bulb and irrigate the other nostril the same way. It's best to use one full bulb for each side of the nose.

You know you're irrigating correctly if mucus is flushed out the front of the nose. You may need to blow your nose afterward to clear the loosened mucus. When you're done, you'll notice you can breathe much better through your nose.

Nasal irrigation may feel unusual the first time you try it—kind of like getting water in your nose when you jumped into a pool as a kid. But once you get the hang of it, it's very soothing.

## Nasal Irrigation FAQs

Here are answers to frequently asked questions about nasal irrigation.

### Should I Inhale as I Squirt?

Inhaling is not necessary; the pressure from the bulb is enough to force the water into your nasal cavity. But there's no harm in inhaling if that's your preference.

### Where Does the Water Go?

Most of the water goes into your nasal cavity, including the middle meatus, and then flows right out. Unless you've had sinus surgery to enlarge your ostia, water does not usually enter your sinuses. But it's not a problem if a little water does get into the sinuses; it just drains back out.

### I Feel a Burning or Stinging Sensation—Can This Be Eliminated?

Some people find nasal irrigation stings a little. Fine-tuning the saltwater solution in two ways may reduce or eliminate this sensation:

- **Adjust salinity.** You add salt to the water because the mucus in your nose is inherently salty, and you want to replicate mucus's natural salinity. Believe it or not, irrigation would sting more if you used plain water. Because individual salinity varies, you may need to play around with the salt level to find what works for you. Reducing the amount of salt to just half a teaspoon eliminates the burning sensation for most people.
- **Adjust alkalinity.** Mucus is slightly less acidic than water, and the imbalance can cause stinging in some patients. You can remedy this disparity by adding half a teaspoon of baking soda to the irrigating solution (in addition to the salt).

## Is It Preferable to Use Distilled or Boiled Water Instead of Tap Water?

No. Although it does no harm to use water that has been purified or sterilized, it's not really necessary. Regular tap water is clean enough that it will not introduce harmful bacteria. Remember, your nose and sinuses are not sterile to begin with.

## Do I Need to Use a Special Type of Salt?

No. Although some doctors recommend using kosher salt or pickling salt for nasal irrigation because it's purer than regular table salt, the same salt you use at your dinner table works fine.

## Can I Irrigate More than Twice a Day?

Certainly. Twice a day, after brushing your teeth, is a good starting point. Ideally, irrigating just before you go to bed will enable you to breathe freely long enough to help you fall asleep. But during the overnight hours, mucus will eventually build up, so you want to irrigate again upon waking to clear out what's accumulated overnight.

Feel free to add more irrigations throughout the day. The beauty of irrigation is that no drugs are involved, so there are few or no side effects. Many people add a third irrigation, at lunchtime. Those whose sinuses produce an unusually large volume of mucus may irrigate even more frequently. As long as you don't get carried away and start rinsing your nose at movie theaters and wedding receptions, you can irrigate as often as you'd like.

## Can I Irrigate During a Sinus Infection?

Yes. To compensate for the increased mucus production during an infection, you may even want to irrigate more often than you usually do.

## Should I Clean the Bulb?

Yes. It's a good idea to wash the bulb weekly with soap and water to clean off any debris and excess salt that accumulates. You can also boil the bulb for a few minutes once a month, to clean the inside. With regular use and cleaning, eventually the bulb will start to crack. When this happens, toss it and buy a new one.

## Can I Stop and Start Irrigations?

Yes. It's perfectly acceptable to irrigate only when you feel the need. Many people rinse their nose exclusively when mucus builds up and congestion develops, such as during allergy season or an infection. Even if you opt for daily irrigation, there are no major drawbacks from occasionally skipping a day. Just be aware that thick mucus can dry up and form crusts, which may be more difficult to clean once you resume irrigating.

## Alternatives to the Bulb Syringe

The bulb syringe works fine for most people. I recommend it because it's easy to obtain and use, and it's inexpensive. However, an ever-growing array of products exists for nasal irrigation (see Figure 7.2 and Table 7.1). Some offer advantages in terms of convenience; others provide more efficient methods to clear thick mucus. All these products are effective when used properly, so as long as they work for you, you really can't go wrong.

### Squeeze Bottles

Several companies make plastic squeeze bottles specifically designed to squirt water up your nose. The technique is similar to using a bulb syringe.

Some squeeze bottles come prefilled with saline solution, and others come with packets of salt that you add to warm water. These products may include the words "isotonic" or "hypertonic" on their labels; *isotonic* means the water is intended to be as salty as your mucus, while *hypertonic* means it's even saltier. I recommend the isotonic variety. Some people believe hypertonic solutions may work better for very thick mucus, but I haven't found that to be the case among my patients. In addition, the label may say "buffered"—this means baking soda has been added to adjust the solution's alkalinity.

The advantage of spray bottles is convenience; assuming the solution does not sting, you never have to worry about adding too little or too much salt or baking soda. The disadvantage is expense. The initial purchase is costlier than a bulb syringe, and there's the additional expense of having to buy refills of solution or packets.

## Neti Pots

Neti pots are small cups that look like a genie's lamp, with a handle on one end and a spout on the other. The name comes from jala neti, a centuries-old yoga practice in which these pots are used for nasal irrigation.

You fill the neti pot with salt water and tilt your head sideways. While breathing gently through your mouth, you pour the water

**FIGURE 7.2** Irrigation Devices

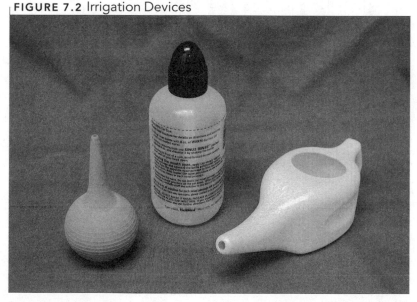

*Devices commonly used for nasal irrigation include (left to right) a bulb syringe, an irrigation bottle, and a neti pot.*

**TABLE 7.1** Nasal Irrigation Products

| Product Category | Availability | Advantages | Disadvantages | Cost* | Brands Available | Website |
|---|---|---|---|---|---|---|
| Bulb syringe | Drugstores, medical supply stores | Low cost | Need for periodic replacement | $ | Generic | |
| Squeeze bottle | Drugstores, Internet | Convenience | Need to reorder salt packets or solution | $$ | Sinus Rinse (comes with salt packets) | neilmed.com |
| | | | | | SaltAire Sinus Relief (comes with saline solution) | saltairesinuswash.com |
| Neti pot | Drugstores, catalogs, Internet | Durability | No water pressure, so may not be effective for thick mucus | $$ | SinuCleanse (comes with salt packets) | sinucleanse.com |
| | | | | | Many types available from small manufacturers | netipot.org healthandyoga.com apeacefulco.com |
| Waterpik and other motorized irrigators | Drugstores, department stores, Internet | High water pressure benefits people with very thick mucus and crusts | High cost | $$$ (irrigator plus attachment) | Waterpik | waterpik.com |
| | | | | | RinoFlow | rinoflow.com |
| | | | | | Hydro Pulse | hydromedonline.com |

*Cost: $ = under $5; $$ = $5 to $30; $$$ = $30 to $150.

into the top nostril. The water flows through the nasal cavity and drains out the bottom nostril. Then you tilt your head the other way and repeat the procedure, pouring the salt water through the other nostril.

Neti pots used to be hard to find in the United States, but in the past few years they have become widely available, in ceramic, stainless steel, or plastic. An advantage of the neti pot is that it's more durable than a bulb syringe; as long as you boil it occasionally, you can use the same one for years. The disadvantage is that it lacks the force of a bulb syringe, so it may not be so effective if you have very thick mucus.

## Waterpik and Other Motorized Devices

A number of plug-in devices are available for those who prefer a high-tech approach to nasal irrigation. The most well-known is the Waterpik, which is commonly used to clean the gums and teeth. Most stores that carry this unit also sell an attachment called Gentle Sinus Rinse (also known as a Grossan tip) for nasal irrigation. You add salt to the water reservoir and hold the tip of the irrigator to your nostrils. Because the Waterpik delivers a relatively forceful, intermittent stream of salt water, many individuals find these devices very helpful to clear thick mucus and crusts.

## Alkalol

No matter what type of irrigation device you use, if you have very thick mucus, it may be helpful to add a mucus-thinning agent to your saltwater solution. One example of such an agent is a liquid called Alkalol. It contains several ingredients designed to thin mucus and soothe nasal passages, including alcohol, baking soda, eucalyptus, menthol, and camphor. Alkalol is available over the counter at drugstores and via the Internet. Although the directions recommend using it at full strength or mixing it fifty-fifty with the usual saltwater solution, many of my patients find it works well when mixed at one-quarter strength, and it lasts longer that way.

## What's Next

Whatever product you choose, you'll be amazed at how much of a difference nasal irrigation can make. Many people find this simple technique provides tremendous relief from sinusitis symptoms and reduces the frequency of infections.

But bulb syringes, squeeze bottles, and neti pots aren't the only simple purchases that can make a difference in your struggle with sinusitis. In the next chapter, we'll look at some products available at most drugstores—including humidifiers, nasal tape, and saline sprays—that may also help.

# CHAPTER 8

# A Trip to the Drugstore: Products for Your Nose and Sinuses

As effective as irrigations are at relieving nasal symptoms, most people with sinusitis need additional measures to obtain the relief they seek. Your local drugstore carries dozens of products intended to help people with sinusitis and other congestion-related ailments. Table 8.1 provides information on some of these products, including brand names, benefits and drawbacks, and general pricing information. Whether a particular product will help you depends on your specific symptoms and their cause. Let's take a look at what's available.

## Humidifiers

A humidifier can make a huge difference if you live in a hot, desert climate (where the air is always naturally dry) or in a cold climate (where the indoor air is artificially dry because the heating system produces "dry heat"). Problems from dry indoor heating are usually worst at night, when people often bump up the thermostat a few degrees to compensate for the lower outdoor temperature. With the windows shut and the heat on, the humid-

**TABLE 8.1** Drugstore Products That May Reduce Sinusitis Symptoms

| Product Category | Manufacturers/ Brands Available | Symptoms Treated | Benefits | Disadvantages/ Drawbacks | Cost* |
|---|---|---|---|---|---|
| Humidifiers | Bemis, Hamilton Beach, Holmes, Honeywell, Hunter, Kenmore, Vornado, others | Nasal dryness, congestion, postnasal drip | Combat effects of dry indoor heating systems, excellent in cold climates, work all night at bedside | Need proper cleaning | $$$ |
| Nasal tape | Breathe Right | Congestion | Provides instant relief | Effective only for narrowed nasal valve, visible to others | $$ |
| Mechanical dilators | Breathe with Eez, Sinus Cones | Congestion | Provide instant relief, not visible to others | Effective only for narrowed nasal valve, can be uncomfortable | $$ |
| Saline sprays | Ayr, Breathe Right, Entsol, Ocean, Rhinaris | Nasal dryness, congestion | Inexpensive, good on airline flights | Less effective for thick mucus, short-lasting effect, requires repeated use | $ |
| Moisturizing sprays and gels | Ayr, Breathe-ease, Breathe Right, Entsol, Ponaris, Rhinaris, Snore Relief | Nasal dryness, congestion, postnasal drip | Longer lasting effect than saline sprays | Cost more than saline sprays | $$ |

*Cost: $ = under $10; $$ = $10 to $30; $$$ = $30 to $150.

ity in a home can drop to 20 percent, compared to the optimal level of 40 to 50 percent obtained when the windows are open.

The symptoms you have throughout the day are largely determined by what happens at night. If you're inhaling extremely dry air with every breath for seven or eight straight hours, you're setting yourself up for sinus problems. Dryness causes mucus to thicken and form crusts, leading to nasal congestion and sinus obstruction.

A bedside humidifier is an effective way to add moisture to the air and reduce congestion and coughing. You can buy a basic model at a drugstore or hardware store for less than $50, with fancier models costing two or three times that amount.

It's best to place the humidifier on your nightstand, so it's close to your head while you sleep. With the addition of this simple device, many people find they no longer wake up with a blocked nose and thick mucus in their throat. Some even buy a second humidifier to place near their desk at work. Although not as critical as using one at night, this additional source of moist air during the day can also help.

While I enthusiastically recommend humidifiers, I must emphasize the importance of keeping them clean. Follow the manufacturers' directions about changing the filter and cleaning the inside regularly. A humidifier can do more harm than good if it becomes contaminated with mold and bacteria—the last thing you need is a device that circulates sinus-irritating microorganisms around your bedroom.

One final note. Patients often ask me whether they should buy a warm- or cool-mist humidifier. Warm-mist models boil the water before it's released, and they tend to stay clean a bit longer but are more expensive. Apart from the cleaning issue, warm-mist models are of no particular benefit for people with sinusitis. The extra warmth of the inhaled mist can help individuals with respiratory problems involving the throat and lungs (such as babies with croup). But you need moisture, and cool mist is just as moist as warm mist.

## Nasal Tape

You've probably seen pro football players on the sidelines wearing odd-looking pieces of tape across the bridge of their noses. Although the strips' effectiveness in enhancing athletic performance through better nasal breathing is doubtful, they can help relieve nasal obstruction in a subset of sinusitis sufferers whose obstruction is caused by a very specific problem: a narrowed nasal valve.

What's a nasal valve? Well, it's not the solid bone part at the bridge and it's not the soft cartilage at the tip. Rather, it's the firmer tissue in the middle third of your nose that collapses inward slightly when you take a deep breath. In some people, the nasal valve is narrower than normal, making it hard for inhaled air to get by. Such narrowing may result from swelling caused by allergies or from an anatomical defect, such as an old nasal fracture or a deviated septum.

Each nasal strip consists of two flat parallel bands of plastic embedded in a special adhesive pad. When placed across the nose, the bands lift the skin upward and outward, pulling open the flexible cartilage walls and widening the nasal valve.

If you have a narrowed nasal valve, these strips can definitely help you breathe better. Unfortunately, most congestion results from swelling of the turbinates or other nasal membranes in a different location than the nasal valve. If you are unsure of the source of your congestion and have problems sleeping at night because of blocked nasal breathing, then you may want to give nasal strips a try. The worst that can happen is they won't work. And if they do help you at night, you can also wear them during the day, as long as you don't mind looking like an NFL linebacker.

## Mechanical Dilators

Several other mechanical devices are available that widen the nasal valve. Usually made of plastic, these products are inserted just inside the nostril. Many patients find them uncomfortable, but a few swear by them. As with nasal strips, they'll only relieve congestion if you have a narrowed nasal valve.

## Saline Sprays

For people who experience nasal dryness, saline sprays are a convenient way to supplement nasal irrigation and humidifiers. These sprays come in small plastic squeeze bottles containing a saltwater solution and some preservatives. Numerous brands are available.

Saline sprays are most helpful for people with rhinitis (inflammation of the nose) caused by prolonged exposure to dry air. By moistening the inside of your nose, they ease the discomfort resulting from nasal dryness. Like humidifiers, saline sprays loosen the thick mucus associated with a dry nose, so it's easier to clear and less likely to obstruct the nose and sinuses. Saline sprays are also good on long airplane flights, where the recycled air is often very dry.

Saline sprays are relatively inexpensive, but you'll go through bottles very quickly if you use them regularly. If cost is an issue, you may wish to make your own saltwater solution.

## Moisturizing Sprays and Gels

Some manufacturers augment traditional nasal saline sprays with ingredients designed to prolong their moisturizing effect, soothe inflamed membranes, and cut through thick mucus. Additives often include menthol, camphor, eucalyptus, and cottonseed oil, as well as essential oils to enhance flavor and aroma, such as peppermint and clove.

Similar to moisturizing sprays, but even thicker and therefore longer lasting, are nasal gels. These products contain many of the same ingredients as moisturizing sprays and may include additional emollients, such as aloe vera. You apply a thin layer just inside your nostril with a finger or Q-tip. As the warmth from your body slowly melts the gel, it flows back to coat the nasal cavity. Because an application of these sprays and gels lasts longer than a spray of saline, they are especially good for combating dryness at night.

## What's Next

If your symptoms don't respond to nasal irrigation or the products described in this chapter, then it's time to take things up a notch and enter the world of over-the-counter and prescription medications. In the next three chapters, I'll help you make sense of the large list of medications available to treat sinusitis, starting with decongestants, mucus-thinning agents, and antihistamines.

CHAPTER 9

# Cold and Allergy Medications: Which Ones Can Help Your Sinusitis?

No doubt about it, the multitude of over-the-counter and pre-scription medications available to treat nasal and sinus symptoms can be intimidating. With similar-sounding names and literally hundreds of drug combinations to choose from, it's a cruel irony that you usually end up having to navigate this maze of medica-tions when you feel least up to it. The good news is that once you're familiar with the major drug categories, finding the right product for your symptoms is less confusing than it initially seems.

I should point out that none of the drugs I'm about to discuss are specifically intended to treat chronic sinusitis. Rather, most are approved to treat symptoms of colds and allergies. But because sinusitis sufferers often have similar symptoms, such as congestion and a runny nose, these drugs can be helpful if you have sinusitis.

There are five major categories of drugs relevant to nasal symptoms: decongestants, mucus-thinning agents, antihistamines, pain relievers, and cough suppressants. Table 9.1 includes key information on drugs in the first three categories. Once we've

**TABLE 9.1** Cold and Allergy Medications That May Also Be Used for Sinusitis

| If You Have ... | ... Consider Taking | Brands Available* | Active Ingredient | Most Common Side Effects/ Warnings |
|---|---|---|---|---|
| Congestion | Decongestants | Sudafed | Pseudoephedrine | May raise blood pressure or cause heart palpitations, jitteriness, or insomnia |
| Thick mucus, postnasal drip | Mucus-thinning agents | Mucinex, Humibid LA** | Guaifenesin | Uncommon |
| Allergy symptoms, such as drainage, itchy eyes and nose, and sneezing | Sedating antihistamines | Benadryl | Diphenhydramine | Drowsiness, dry mouth |
| | | Chlor-Trimeton | Chlorpheniramine | |
| | | Dimetane | Brompheniramine | |
| | | Tavist | Clemastine | |
| | Nonsedating antihistamines | Alavert | Loratadine | Uncommon |
| | | Allegra** | Fexofenadine | |
| | | Clarinex** | Desloratadine | |
| | | Claritin | Loratadine | |
| | Other | Zyrtec** | Cetirizine | Occasional drowsiness |

\* Generic forms of nonprescription brands also available.
\*\* Available by prescription only.

looked at each individual drug category, we'll talk about combination medications.

## Decongestants

Decongestant medications are available in both spray and pill form. Spray decongestants such as Afrin, Dristan, Vicks, and Neo-Synephrine contain either oxymetazoline or phenylephrine. Although these sprays provide rapid relief of nasal congestion, I do not recommend them for people with chronic sinusitis because they offer a high potential for nasal rebound if used for more than three days (see Chapter 5).

Once you eliminate sprays, you're left with just one over-the-counter decongestant that comes in oral form: pseudoephedrine, the little red pill commonly sold under the brand name Sudafed. It is also available in a variety of generic brands. (Another decongestant, phenylpropanolamine, or PPA, was taken off the market in 2000 because of FDA concerns that it increased the risk of stroke.)

Pseudoephedrine acts by constricting blood vessels, thereby reducing blood flow through mucous membranes in your nose. These membranes shrink, leaving more room in your sinus and nasal passages for air to flow and mucus to drain. So if you're plugged up, taking a decongestant can enable you to breathe again. It can also relieve a sense of facial fullness and congestion.

However, pseudoephedrine has a number of drawbacks. First, it can raise blood pressure, so it's not recommended for people with hypertension. Those taking blood pressure medication should check with their doctor before starting to use it.

Next, pseudoephedrine is a stimulant, so it can make you feel jittery, hyperactive, or anxious. In a small number of people, it can even cause heart palpitations (rapid or extra heartbeats). If this occurs, you should discontinue its use. Pseudoephedrine's stimulant effect can also cause insomnia. If you experience this side effect but find that pseudoephedrine helps control your symptoms, you may wish to take it in the morning and skip the evening dose.

## Mucus-Thinning Agents

Just as pseudoephedrine is the only available oral decongestant, there is just one mucus-thinning agent: guaifenesin. We don't know exactly how it works, but guaifenesin takes thick mucus and makes it more watery, so it's easier to clear from your nose and sinuses. Guaifenesin is also referred to as an expectorant, because it helps people cough up and spit out thick secretions that may collect in the throat or chest.

As long as you take the proper dosage, guaifenesin does not normally have side effects. But there is one critical thing to remember: make sure you're well hydrated when you take it. Your body must have enough water available to achieve the medication's mucus-thinning benefit. It's a good idea to drink an eight-ounce glass of water with each dose.

## Antihistamines

A general consensus exists among physicians that oral decongestants and mucus-thinning agents benefit many patients with sinusitis. By contrast, the role of antihistamines is more controversial. Because antihistamines can dry out your nasal passages and thicken secretions, some doctors believe people with sinusitis should never take them.

I don't share this view. I believe antihistamines do have a role for many people with sinusitis, particularly those whose infections seem to be related to allergies. And even if you don't have a history of environmental allergies, a trial of antihistamines should be considered if pseudoephedrine and guaifenesin haven't provided relief.

Antihistamines act by blocking the release of histamine, a chemical produced by the body in reaction to foreign substances known as allergens. Histamine release triggers a cascade of inflammatory factors that results in the familiar allergy response, including swelling of the nasal membranes, congestion, itching, sneezing, and runny nose.

The effectiveness of these medications varies by individual and by drug. An antihistamine that effectively relieves sinus symptoms in one person may prove totally ineffective for someone else. So if one class or brand of antihistamine doesn't work, it's often worthwhile to try another.

### Oral Antihistamines

Most antihistamines used to treat sinusitis are taken in pill form. There are two types of these oral antihistamines available: sedating and nonsedating.

*Sedating Antihistamines.* Over-the-counter sedating antihistamines include chlorpheniramine (Chlor-Trimeton), diphenhydramine (Benadryl), brompheniramine (Dimetane), and clemas-tine (Tavist). While sedating antihistamines are generally effective, their drawback is that they cross the so-called blood-brain barrier, meaning they enter the brain tissues and can affect the central nervous system. The most common side effect that results is drowsiness, which can affect up to half of patients who take these antihistamines. Some people find antihistamines make them feel spacey when they take them. Another side effect from these med-ications is dryness. In some individuals, the mucous membranes of the mouth and nose become dry and secretions thicken.

The sedating side effect of these antihistamines can also be their benefit. Many patients take antihistamines at nighttime to help them fall asleep while controlling sinusitis symptoms.

**Nonsedating Antihistamines.** Because they do not cross the blood-brain barrier, the newer nonsedating antihistamines are less likely than sedating antihistamines to cause drowsiness and other side effects. Three nonsedating antihistamines are available in oral for-mulations. Loratadine is sold over the counter as Claritin and Alavert. A closely related medication, desloratadine (Clarinex), is available by prescription, as is fexofenadine (Allegra). Although a fourth relatively new antihistamine, cetirizine (Zyrtec), is not con-sidered nonsedating, its incidence of associated drowsiness is rela-tively low.

All four of these antihistamines are available in longer-acting formulations than over-the-counter sedating antihistamines, so you only need to take them once a day. They're also produced in combination with pseudoephedrine, in which case there's a "D" (for decongestant) following the name (see Table 9.2, a little later in the chapter).

## Antihistamine Sprays
One prescription antihistamine, azelastine (Astelin), is available in a nasal spray to be used twice a day. Like other antihistamines, it's intended to reduce swelling and relieve congestion by blocking the allergic cascade triggered by histamine. Azelastine's advantage

is that side effects are minimized because it's applied directly to the nasal passages, with little absorption into the bloodstream. Although it works well for some people with sinusitis and allergies, I've not found it to be as effective as oral antihistamines are for most. Also, it has an unpleasant taste that some people find intolerable.

## Pain Relievers and Cough Suppressants

Along with the three categories I've already discussed, two other types of drugs are commonly combined in cold and allergy medications: pain relievers and cough suppressants.

Pain relievers include aspirin, acetaminophen (Tylenol), and nonsteroidal anti–inflammatory drugs (Advil, Motrin, Aleve), also known as NSAIDs. These medications treat both headache pain and the discomfort described as facial pressure due to blocked sinuses.

The most common nonnarcotic cough suppressant is dextromethorphan, the active ingredient found in Robitussin and other cough medicines. More potent cough suppressants contain narcotics, such as codeine, requiring a prescription. Although coughing is not one of the more common sinusitis symptoms, it does occur when postnasal drip drains into the chest, especially when you are lying down at night.

## Combination Products

Cold and allergy combination products include one or more drugs from each of the five categories we've discussed:

- decongestants
- mucus-thinning agents
- antihistamines
- pain relievers
- cough suppressants

Somewhat like a Chinese menu, you can order à la carte or go for a combo plate. Table 9.2 shows you some of the most common combinations.

When you are choosing a product, your underlying assumption should be that you want to take as little medication as possible, since there's no sense in needlessly exposing yourself to side

TABLE 9.2 Drug Combinations for Sinusitis

| Combination | Brand Names* |
| --- | --- |
| Decongestants + mucus-thinning agents | **OTC**<br>Deconsal II<br>Sinutab Non-Drying<br>Sudafed Non-Drying Sinus<br><br>**Prescription**<br>Entex-PSE<br>Guaifed-PSE |
| Decongestants + pain relievers | **OTC**<br>Sinutab Sinus<br>Sudafed Sinus & Cold<br>Sudafed Sinus Headache<br>Tylenol Sinus Day Non-Drowsy |
| Decongestants + antihistamines | **OTC**<br>Actifed Cold & Allergy<br>Alavert-D<br>Benadryl Allergy & Sinus<br>Benadryl-D Allergy & Sinus<br>Claritin-D<br>Sudafed Sinus & Allergy<br>Sudafed Sinus Nighttime<br>Tavist-D<br><br>**Prescription**<br>Allegra-D<br>Zyrtec-D |
| Decongestants + antihistamines + pain relievers | **OTC**<br>Actifed Cold & Sinus<br>Dimetapp Cold & Allergy<br>Drixoral Cold & Flu<br>Benadryl Allergy & Cold<br>Benadryl Allergy & Sinus Headache<br>Benadryl Severe Allergy & Sinus Headache<br>Sinutab Sinus Allergy<br>Sudafed Sinus Nighttime Plus Pain Relief<br>Tylenol Sinus Night Time |
| Decongestants + antihistamines + mucus-thinning agents | **Prescription**<br>Decon-G |
| Decongestants + pain relievers + mucus-thinning agents | **OTC**<br>Tylenol Sinus Severe Congestion |

* Generic versions of nonprescription brands also available.

effects. Symptoms vary by individual and may change from epi-sode to episode, so you need to do a self-evaluation before decid-ing whether to take a single drug or a combination.

For example, if you have thick mucus but don't feel congested, then you only need guaifenesin. And if you're congested but have thin mucus, then you only need pseudoephedrine. Often, how-ever, congestion and thick mucus go hand in hand. If that's the case, then choose a product that contains both pseudoephedrine and guaifenesin.

As mentioned earlier, antihistamines are most helpful if you have allergies. However, if you've found other remedies are inef-fective, combining an antihistamine with pseudoephedrine may be beneficial.

## Other Medications

Two other medications—both available in spray form—are less commonly used than the medications I've already discussed, but for some people with sinusitis, they can be quite helpful:

- **Cromolyn sodium (NasalCrom).** This over-the-counter medication is called a mast-cell stabilizer. It is intended to reduce postnasal drip and sneezing caused by allergies. Normally, upon entering the nose, an allergen triggers the mast cells that line the nasal passages to release histamines, which cause nasal allergy symptoms. Cromolyn sodium provides a protective layer that shields mast cells from these allergens. It is most helpful when taken in a preventive manner—that is, just before you're exposed to the substance that triggers your nasal allergies.
- **Ipratropium (Atrovent).** This prescription medication is an anticholinergic agent, meaning it dries up the nose. It seems to work best in individuals whose main problem is excessive production of clear nasal mucus out the front of their nose from either allergies or a cold. It's not very

effective for those with thick postnasal drip caused by infected sinuses. Ipratropium is available in spray bottles at two different strengths (0.3 percent and 0.6 percent).

## What's Next

Next, we'll look at nasal steroids, which are some of the most commonly prescribed medications for people with sinusitis.

# CHAPTER 10

# Steroids: A Way to Reduce Inflammation, Congestion, and Polyps

Steroids get a lot of press because of their questionable use by weight lifters and other athletes to enhance performance. But you needn't worry. Those are anabolic steroids, which build muscle; the steroids used to treat nasal and sinus symptoms are an entirely different class of compound known as corticosteroids. Taking them won't enable you to bench-press 350 pounds, but you'll probably find they help you breathe better.

Steroids can be delivered to the nose in two ways: by spray or pill. Either way, they're available only by prescription. Both forms are potent anti–inflammatory agents. Simply put, they reduce swelling. Steroids act by passing through a cell's membranes into its nucleus, stopping the process that causes inflammation at its source.

Steroids are also the most effective tool we have for reducing nasal polyps, short of surgery. Polyps' size tends to vary depending on the individual's place on the Sinusitis Spectrum (see Figure 10.1). Most Locals don't have polyps, but if they do, the polyps tend to be small and located in or near the ostiomeatal complex (OMC). Intermediates often have larger polyps, which arise from

FIGURE 10.1 The Sinusitis Spectrum—Polyps

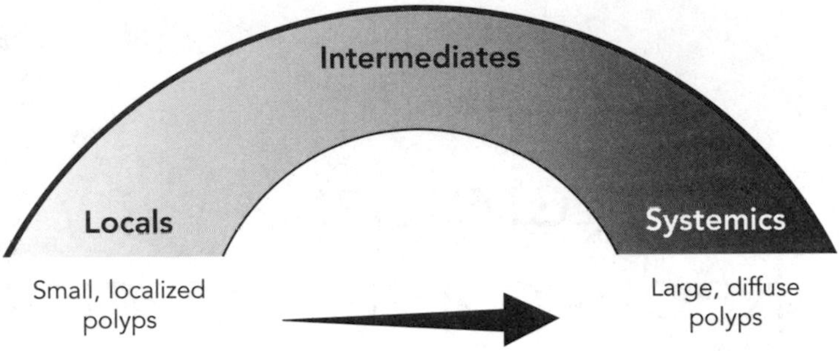

*The location and size of nasal polyps correspond to where a person fits in on the Sinusitis Spectrum.*

the ethmoid sinuses and extend into the nasal cavity. Systemics frequently have large polyps that obstruct all of the sinuses and block nasal breathing.

Most of this chapter focuses on nasal steroid sprays, because they are widely used by people with sinusitis. At the end, I'll address pills (oral steroids), which are used much less frequently due to their side effects.

## Nasal Steroid Sprays

Nasal steroid sprays are a logical and common next step for many sinusitis patients whose symptoms do not respond to over-the-counter treatments. Spraying steroids directly into your nose delivers the steroid in relatively high concentration to the nasal membranes, where it can block inflammation from allergies and other causes. A topical steroid spray can:

• reduce swelling of the turbinates and nasal membranes
• reduce nasal secretions, particularly those due to allergies
• shrink polyps

With swelling reduced and less secretions, you're likely to breathe better. Also, there's a good possibility that the OMC will open up, allowing your sinuses to drain and air to get in and out. In addition, shrinking polyps often means your sense of smell will improve if it's been impaired.

## Nasal Steroid FAQs

Here are answers to frequently asked questions about nasal steroid sprays.

### How Long Does It Take for Steroids to Start Working?

Patients often find they need to use steroid sprays for four or five days before they notice any benefits; unlike with spray decongestants, you should not expect an immediate effect.

### Which Nasal Steroid Should I Use?

Many different steroids are available by prescription. Flonase is the most well-known due to heavy advertising; others include Beconase, Nasacort, Nasarel, Nasonex, Rhinocort, and Vancenase (see Table 10.1).

Although their active ingredients may differ, there is no clear evidence that one steroid spray is superior to any other. However, their effects do vary from person to person. Many of my patients sense no improvement using one brand and find good relief when

**TABLE 10.1** Commonly Prescribed Nasal Steroids

| Name | Active Ingredient |
| --- | --- |
| Beconase, Beconase AQ | Beclomethasone |
| Flonase | Fluticasone |
| Nasacort, Nasacort AQ | Triamcinolone |
| Nasarel | Flunisolide |
| Nasonex | Mometasone |
| Rhinocort Aqua | Budesonide |
| Vancenase, Vancenase AQ | Beclomethasone |

they switch to another. Your doctor will prescribe the steroid spray he or she is most familiar with or believes will be most effective for you. If one spray does not seem to be working after several weeks, talk to your doctor about switching to another brand to see if it makes a difference.

## What Are the Potential Side Effects?

Nasal steroid sprays should not have long-term side effects as long as you take the recommended dose. The active ingredient is absorbed through the nasal membranes in such minute amounts that body functions are unlikely to be disrupted. Steroid sprays are among the most widely prescribed medications in the world, and people have taken them for years, even decades, without problems.

However, two short-term side effects occur in about one in five users: nosebleeds and a burning sensation in the nose. Both problems can usually be avoided if you exercise care when you spray. The trick is to spray toward the outside of your nose, where the turbinates are. If you spray toward the inside, you'll coat the septum, which has a surface rich in blood vessels that may become fragile and rupture with repeated exposure to the steroid.

A good technique for spraying the correct part of your nose is to use your opposite hand for each nostril; in other words, spray your left nostril with your right hand and your right nostril with your left hand. A small study in 2003 by a Georgetown University professor found this sleight of hand nearly eliminated nosebleeds among a group of nasal spray users who had been experiencing two or three per week.

If you do experience nosebleeds, stop taking nasal steroids for two weeks to give the interior of your nose time to heal. Then you can resume use, carefully spraying toward the outside of your nose.

## How Often Should I Use the Spray?

The package includes instructions for a specific medication's recommended usage. In the past, most were used twice a day, but the trend among drug manufacturers is toward once-a-day dosing in which you spray each nostril twice, at a time of your choosing. Some people find it beneficial to split the dosage in half and spread it throughout the day. In other words, you can deliver one spray per nostril in the morning and one spray per nostril in the evening. This tactic spreads out delivery of the active ingredient throughout the day but still provides the same total of four sprays each day, so there's no risk of increased side effects.

## Is It OK if I Skip Sprays on Days When I'm Not Congested?

For maximum effectiveness, you should use steroid sprays every day. However, it's not dangerous to skip days or stop and start sprays—it just may take a few days for their beneficial effects to kick in again.

Also, people with seasonal allergies often only use steroid sprays during the spring and fall when their symptoms flare up. That's fine.

## Oral Steroids

If nasal sprays are not effective, your doctor may prescribe oral steroids. Two are available—prednisone and methylprednisolone (known by the brand name Medrol)—with similar effectiveness and side effect profiles.

First, the good news. Oral steroids are powerful and highly effective in blocking inflammation of the nose and sinuses. Most people find they breathe much better and have less postnasal drip within twenty-four hours of their first dose.

Oral steroids also are highly effective at reducing large polyps. At a certain point, polyps get so large that nasal sprays are no longer effective. A short regimen of oral steroids can often shrink polyps enough that nasal steroid sprays will begin working again.

Now the bad news. Because oral steroids circulate throughout your body, long-term side effects are a major issue. Prolonged use can lead to osteoporosis with weakened bones, thinning of the skin with easy bruising, and a compromised immune system with susceptibility to infection, as well as cataracts, stomach ulcers, fluid retention, and a host of other serious side effects.

When taken as a short course of less than a week, steroids only rarely have side effects, although some people do get insomnia or an upset stomach. But long-term use suppresses the adrenal glands' ability to secrete natural steroids (such as cortisol) that are needed during periods of stress. Therefore, when oral steroids are prescribed for more than one week, they are usually not stopped abruptly but by a gradual decrease in the daily dose. Tapering allows the adrenal glands to ramp up the body's natural secretion of cortisol.

I advise patients against taking more than three courses of oral steroids per year. Along with the increased risk of side effects, repeated use often means a higher dose is required to achieve the same positive effects. Oral steroids are neither a solution nor a cure for most people's sinusitis, but they offer the best nonsurgical means of controlling symptoms for some Intermediates and Systemics.

## What's Next

Steroids in spray or pill form are often used in conjunction with antibiotics. Next, we'll look at the many different antibiotics used to combat sinusitis.

# 11

# Antibiotics: The Mainstay of Sinusitis Treatment

Physicians prescribe hundreds of millions of dollars worth of antibiotics each year for people with sinusitis. These bacteria-slaying medications generally are effective. In most cases, antibiotics eliminate the infection-causing bacteria, allowing inflamed nasal mucous membranes to shrink and your sinuses to drain.

Unfortunately, it's not always so straightforward. Antibiotics sometimes fail to do away with the offending bacteria or provide only temporary improvement, with a return of symptoms as soon as you stop taking the medication. Also, antibiotics can be expensive and they have side effects.

So let's take a look at the world of antibiotics for sinusitis: how they work, the different types that are available, and their benefits and drawbacks.

## Symptom Relief

Taken in pill form, antibiotics are absorbed in the stomach and distributed through the body via the bloodstream. As a result, they are effective in areas of the body that have a good blood supply. The well-vascularized mucous membranes inside your sinuses can deliver an adequate dose of antibiotic to rapidly kill bacteria for most sinus infections. You typically notice an improvement in symptoms within forty-eight hours. Pain subsides, swelling goes down, and thick mucus becomes thinner. You may note a temporary increase in postnasal drip—a sign the antibiotic is working.

However, with a severe infection that fills a sinus cavity with mucus or pus, there may not be an adequate blood supply in the center of the sinus to deliver the antibiotic. Bacteria living in the fluid may continue to multiply, so it takes weeks, instead of days, to kill enough bacteria to allow the sinuses to fully open and drain the offending microorganisms.

Also, antibiotics sometimes fail because bacteria are resistant to them (see the sidebar "Sinusitis and Antibiotic Resistance"). If an infection fails to show signs of improvement after ten days or if an infection goes away but comes back within a few weeks, your doctor has two options: having you take the first antibiotic again for a longer period of time or trying a different antibiotic that kills a larger variety of bacteria (what's known as a broad-spectrum antibiotic). For chronic sinus infections, it's not unusual for an antibiotic to be prescribed for three or more weeks. To improve the likelihood of success, it's important to complete the full course.

## Choosing an Antibiotic

From a physician's perspective, selecting the "best" antibiotic for a given case of sinusitis can be a guessing game. Why is this so?

First, there's an appalling lack of information on the effectiveness of different antibiotics for the treatment of chronic sinusitis. You may be surprised to learn that the U.S. Food and Drug Administration (FDA) has yet to approve even one antibiotic for the treatment of chronic sinusitis. Many antibiotics *are* approved to treat acute sinusitis, and doctors simply prescribe these same

## Sinusitis and Antibiotic Resistance

One important factor your physician takes into account when prescribing an antibiotic is bacterial resistance. On a societal level, the more an antibiotic is prescribed, the more likely bacteria are to develop resistance to that antibiotic.

Researchers are engaged in an ongoing battle against the army of bacteria; newly developed antibiotics are initially highly effective but lose effectiveness over time as resistance develops. Certain bacterial infections can be fatal, particularly if they reach vital organs, such as the lungs or brain, so maintaining an arsenal of effective antibiotics is a serious global health issue.

The biggest problem contributing to resistance is unnecessary use of antibiotics. For example, they're often needlessly prescribed for the common cold, which is caused by a virus, not bacteria. Antibiotics are not effective against viruses. Sinusitis, on the other hand, *is* caused by bacterial infection, so antibiotics have a legitimate role in its treatment.

antibiotics for chronic sinusitis. As a result, there's little economic incentive for drug manufacturers to seek government approval—a difficult and expensive proposition, because chronic sinusitis is not one disease but a spectrum of many diseases. Therefore, we don't have scientific data demonstrating one antibiotic's superiority over another for chronic sinusitis, nor do we know the optimal dose or dose duration.

A second treatment dilemma relates to the offending bacteria. Recall from Chapter 5 that one of three bacteria causes most cases of acute sinusitis: *Streptococcus pneumoniae, Haemophilus influenzae,* and *Moraxella catarrhalis.* Chronic sinusitis is more complicated. There are more potential culprits, and infections are often polymicrobial, meaning two or more bacteria contribute to the infection.

We know that *Staphylococcus aureus* (also referred to as *Staph aureus*, or simply as *staph*) is the critter found most often when cultures of chronic sinus infections are taken, arising in about half of all cases. A host of other bacteria with strange-sounding names may also be present, including *Pseudomonas*, *Klebsiella*, *Peptostreptococcus*, *Fusobacterium*, and *Bacteroides*.

It's not even that uncommon to find *Escherichia coli* (*E. coli*) growing in chronically infected sinuses. You may remember that bacterium from 1993, when hamburger meat contaminated with *E. coli* caused several fatalities at fast-food restaurants. Fortunately, it's not the same strain of *E. coli* that causes sinus infections, which is relatively easy to treat with proper antibiotics.

Because of the large variety of bacteria that can cause a chronic infection, culture-directed therapy is the most accurate way to select the proper antibiotic. In cases where the ENT doctor sees pus flowing from a sinus during an endoscopic examination, a sample can be taken with a small Q-tip. This sample is immediately placed on a culture plate and incubated. Five to seven days later, a lab technician identifies the bacteria that have grown and runs tests to see which antibiotics are effective against them. Armed with this information, the ENT doctor can prescribe an antibiotic that has a high likelihood of working.

## Classes of Antibiotics

There are four major classes of antibiotics used to treat chronic sinusitis—penicillins, cephalosporins, macrolides, and quinolones—as well as a few other minor categories. Table 11.1 shows you the generic and brand names of many of these antibiotics.

### Penicillins

Old-fashioned penicillin is no longer used for sinusitis, because it has lost its effectiveness against numerous bacteria. Instead, we now use amoxicillin, a variant of penicillin. Amoxicillin is usu-

**TABLE 11.1** Antibiotics Used to Treat Sinusitis

| Class | Examples | Brand Name | Cost* |
|---|---|---|---|
| Penicillins | Amoxicillin | (Generic) | $ |
| | Amoxicillin + clavulanate | Augmentin | $$ |
| Cephalosporins | Cephalexin | Keflex | $ |
| | Cefdinir | Omnicef | $$ |
| | Cefixime | Suprax | $$ |
| | Cefpodoxime | Vantin | $$ |
| | Cefuroxime | Ceftin | $$ |
| Macrolides | Erythromycin | (Generic) | $ |
| | Azithromycin | Zithromax | $$ |
| | Clarithromycin | Biaxin | $$ |
| | Telithromycin | Ketek | $$ |
| Quinolones | Ciprofloxacin | Cipro | $$$ |
| | Gatifloxacin | Tequin | $$$ |
| | Levofloxacin | Levaquin | $$$ |
| | Moxifloxacin | Avelox | $$$ |

*Cost: $ = low cost; $$ = moderate cost; $$$ = expensive.

ally effective, but about one-third of patients will have resistant bacteria. Even so, because of its low cost and minimal side effects, amoxicillin is often the first antibiotic prescribed when someone is diagnosed with chronic sinusitis.

If amoxicillin fails—or if a physician believes it might—a common alternative is Augmentin, which combines amoxicillin with clavulanate, a drug that inhibits an enzyme that would ordinarily render amoxicillin inactive. A ten- to twenty-one-day course of Augmentin is effective treatment for most people with chronic sinusitis who develop an infection.

## Cephalosporins

Cephalosporins are a good alternative to penicillins for the treatment of sinusitis; they are commonly used for cases of chronic sinusitis that don't respond to amoxicillin or Augmentin. Cephalosporins are effective against *Staph aureus* about 90 percent of the time. Because staph is a common source of postoperative infection, a course of cephalosporin is commonly prescribed immediately following sinus surgery.

## Macrolides

Macrolides are a powerful class of antibiotics known for their high effectiveness in patients with sinusitis. They are useful for patients with an allergy to penicillin or amoxicillin. Zithromax and Ketek (which actually belongs to a similar class of antibiotics called ketolides) are available in prepackaged five-day courses for acute flare-ups.

## Quinolones

Quinolones are another powerful class of broad-spectrum antibiotics. They are particularly effective against what are known as gram-negative bacteria, such as *Pseudomonas*, which can be the cause of resistant sinus infections. For this reason, they're usually used as a last resort, when a sinus infection hasn't responded to other classes of antibiotics.

## Others

A few other antibiotics are also used for sinusitis. The combination of trimethoprim and sulfamethoxazole (Septra, Bactrim) is effective but contains sulfa, which is a common cause of allergic reactions, some of which can be serious. Clindamycin (Cleocin) is particularly active against a robust type of bacteria known as anaerobes, which do not need oxygen to survive. With prolonged use, this antibiotic can cause a severe form of diarrhea. Linezolid (Zyvox) is effective in treating sinusitis caused by a resistant form of staph (called methicillin-resistant *Staph aureus*, or MRSA) but is extremely expensive, so it's reserved for the most difficult cases.

## Minimizing Side Effects

All antibiotics put you at risk for side effects, with the broad-spectrum antibiotics tending to have more severe side effects. Your doctor will likely discuss side effects for any antibiotic he or she prescribes. Rather than cover every side effect here, I'll discuss the most common ones:

- **Allergic reactions.** True allergic reactions in which people's immune systems are triggered into action when they take antibiotics are rare, accounting for only 5 to 10 percent of all side effects. But these reactions can be severe. The most serious allergic reaction involves the onset of hives, swelling of the throat, and difficulty breathing shortly after taking the medication. These symptoms, known as anaphylaxis, are similar to those that occur in people with severe allergies to peanuts or bee stings and require immediate treatment in an emergency room.

  A more common but less serious allergic reaction from antibiotics is the development of a rash. Most rashes occur within a few days of starting the medication. If one occurs, stop taking the antibiotic immediately and inform your doctor.
- **Stomach problems.** Gastrointestinal disorders, including nausea and diarrhea, are the most common side effect of antibiotics. Such problems are more common with cephalosporins, macrolides, and quinolones than with penicillins.

  Diarrhea can occur because in addition to killing the bacteria in your sinuses, antibiotics do away with bacteria in your bowel that help you digest food. GI side effects tend to be worse on an empty stomach, so taking antibiotics with food can help you avoid or lessen these side effects. Eating a six-ounce cup of yogurt once or twice a day, which replenishes bacteria that aid in digestion, can also be helpful.
- **Yeast infection in women.** Antibiotics also may alter the balance of microorganisms that normally reside in the vagina. Antibiotics suppress bacteria that have an antifungal effect, resulting in an overgrowth of yeast. Antifungal

medications to treat such yeast infections are available over the counter in topical ointments and by prescription in pill form.

- **Sensitivity to sunlight.** While taking a quinolone antibiotic, your skin is unusually susceptible to sunlight. If you're exposed to the sun while taking Cipro or a similar antibiotic, you may suffer a particularly bad sunburn, so be sure to wear a hat and use sunscreen.
- **Unpleasant taste.** Some macrolides, such as Biaxin, can produce a metallic taste.
- **Drug interactions.** Antibiotics may interact with other drugs you're taking, particularly blood pressure, blood-thinning, and seizure medications. Always inform your physician of any medications you take.
- **Effects on pregnancy.** All medications, including antibiotics, present a risk during pregnancy. Your obstetrician can advise you on which antibiotics are considered safest during pregnancy.

## Short- and Long-Term Dosing Regimens

A typical course of antibiotics for sinusitis lasts from ten to fourteen days. For more severe infections, the course can be extended to three to six weeks. However, in some circumstances, patients may benefit from antibiotic regimens that are either shorter or longer than the typical course.

On the short end are the newer, powerful antibiotics such as Zithromax and Ketek that come in three- and five-day packages. Such short-dosing regimens are effective for people with acute sinusitis as well as those with chronic sinusitis who experience acute flare-ups. However, they may be less effective for individuals with severe infections.

At the other extreme is a low-dose, long-term strategy, which may be appropriate for patients who continue to develop sinus infections even after repeated courses of antibiotics for conventional durations. Such regimens involve half the normal daily dosage and last for two to six months. In theory, keeping the bacteria count down for a long stretch allows time for inflamed mucous membranes to heal. The sinuses can then drain better, and the likelihood of future infections is reduced.

Physicians started using this tactic based on its success among children with persistent ear infections. The potential drawback is that bacteria may develop resistance to the antibiotic, so the risk of this side effect must be carefully weighed against the potential benefit.

## Topical and Intravenous Antibiotics

Although antibiotics are usually prescribed in pill form, they don't have to be. In special circumstances, they may be more effective when administered topically or intravenously.

### Topical Antibiotics

In theory, topical application of antibiotics directly into the nasal and sinus cavities makes a lot of sense, because the medication is applied in a relatively high dose where it's needed. Furthermore, side effects should be less than with oral antibiotics, because the medication does not pass through the stomach or bloodstream.

In years past, you could have your local drugstore prepare a nasal spray from a powdered antibiotic mixed with saline. Nowadays, such compounding is too time-consuming and not cost-effective for most pharmacists. Instead, private companies offer this service. With a doctor's prescription, they create an antibiotic solution and ship it to you with a nebulizer, which delivers the medication in a suspension of tiny droplets inhaled through the nose. If you frequently use antibiotics, you may wish to ask your physician about this method. Companies active in this area include SinusPharmacy (which markets a device under the name Sinu-NEB) and SinusDynamics (which calls its nebulizer SinusAero).

Some antibiotics are available as ointments that can be applied inside the nose (see the sidebar "Feeling Crusty? Try an Antibiotic Ointment").

## Feeling Crusty? Try an Antibiotic Ointment

Most antibiotics are available by prescription only, but a few are available over the counter as ointments. You'll find them in your drugstore's first-aid section, and that's what they're primarily used for—minor cuts, scrapes, and burns. Common varieties include bacitracin (often labeled as bacitracin zinc) or Neosporin (which contains a mixture of three antibiotics—bacitracin, neomycin, and polymyxin—and is also available as a generic).

Antibiotic ointments are particularly beneficial for people who develop nasal crusts caused by a combination of dried mucus and bacteria. Such crusts are more than an annoyance—they can hamper breathing and are often a sign the nose is colonized with staph. Applying an antibiotic ointment with a Q-tip just inside the nostril twice a day will cut down on the number of bacteria, usually eliminating the crusts. Because these ointments enhance nasal moisture, they can also help minimize nasal crusting caused by excessive nasal dryness. If crusts persist, your doctor can prescribe a stronger topical antibiotic, such as mupirocin (Bactroban).

### Intravenous Antibiotics

Intravenous (IV) administration of antibiotics is only considered for the most severe sinusitis cases. The two most common scenarios are:

- people who do not respond to oral antibiotic therapy but are not good candidates for surgery
- people whose infection spreads from the sinuses to surrounding tissue in the skin, eyes, or brain

IV administration increases the medication's effectiveness, because the level of antibiotic in the blood is higher than it would be with oral administration. Cases requiring IV administration may be handled by an infectious disease specialist in consultation with an ENT specialist.

Although IV administration often starts in a hospital, where the patient can be monitored for the initial dose, it continues at home, where a visiting nurse can provide assistance. Patients can usually resume most daily activities, taking breaks to administer the antibiotic two to four times a day. In some cases, the patient wears a pump that automatically administers the dosage throughout the day. Courses of therapy usually range from ten days to six weeks.

## What's Next

Next, we'll consider how everyday issues, such as diet, smoking and drinking, and the work environment, can affect your sinuses.

# CHAPTER 12

# Diet and Lifestyle: How Everyday Decisions Can Affect Your Sinuses

For most people, few things are more innocuous than a glass of milk. But for some people with sinusitis, this staple of Americana can have a big impact. In this chapter, we'll examine how milk and other elements of your diet can affect your sinus symptoms. We'll also explore problems at your workplace that can lead to headaches and nasal blockage, including the phenomenon known as sick building syndrome.

## Food Allergies: Milk and Wheat

Although food allergies that trigger sinusitis are relatively rare, they do occur often enough that I'm always on the lookout for them in people whose symptoms cannot be explained by more common causes. The tip-off that such an allergy may be present is when postnasal drip is the primary symptom. If you are particularly bothered by such drainage—or constant collection of phlegm in the back of the throat, especially upon awakening— you may well have a food allergy and not even be aware of it.

What causes food allergies is not well understood, but it's clear that when certain people eat specific foods, undesirable reactions occur. In some cases, such as allergies to shellfish or peanuts, these effects can be immediate, resulting in hives or swelling of the face or throat. In severe cases, these allergic reactions can be life-threatening.

In most cases, however, the effects are more subtle. Symptoms have a gradual onset and are less marked, to the point where people often do not make the connection between the food and the subsequent reaction it causes.

Milk and wheat are the two foods that most commonly cause the allergic reaction that leads to excess mucus production and troublesome postnasal drip. This drainage can also block the nose, impairing breathing and blocking the sinus ostia, prompting an infection.

Diagnosing food allergies can be a bit tricky, as there is no standardized approach used by all allergists and test results can be unreliable. Some favor skin testing similar to that used to detect pollen and dust allergies; minute amounts of the food are placed just beneath the skin to see if any reaction occurs. Others use a blood test called RAST to look for antibodies to food proteins in the blood.

The best way to determine if you have such an allergy is an elimination diet; in other words, you stop eating the suspect food for a period of time and see if that makes a difference. I recommend a trial of at least two weeks, and four weeks is ideal—if you can hold out that long, then you'll know with some certainty whether you're really allergic.

During the trial, you have to be very strict in your diet. With milk, you need to cut out not just the milk you drink, but all products containing even small quantities of milk. That includes cheese, yogurt, and many baked goods. You'd be surprised at how many products contain small amounts of milk, including many breads, sauces, and salad dressings. You'll have to check labels to be sure products are milk-free.

One final milk note. It's the protein component in the milk, not the fat, that causes the increase in mucus production. So simply switching to nonfat milk, while perhaps good for your heart and waistline, won't affect mucus production.

With wheat and wheat-based products, such as bread and pasta, the source of the problem is also a protein—in this case, one called gluten. Again, eliminating wheat for two to four weeks should reveal whether you have this allergy.

People with sinus problems who truly are allergic to milk or wheat often see dramatic symptom improvement when they eliminate the offending food. Many of my patients whose postnasal drip did not improve with conventional medications (including antihistamines, steroid sprays, and antibiotics) have reported a huge decrease in the amount of mucus produced by their nose within a few weeks of starting an elimination diet.

While milk and wheat can worsen sinus symptoms, certain spicy foods may actually reduce them (see the sidebar "Hot Peppers, Anyone?").

## Hot Peppers, Anyone?

Anyone who has taken a bite out of a hot chili pepper knows how the sudden burning sensation can trigger the eyes to water and the nose and sinuses to open up and drain. This intense reaction is caused by capsaicin, a chemical found in many hot, spicy foods.

Capsaicin is also available in capsule and spray form. Several researchers have looked at whether a regular dose relieves congestion and promotes sinus drainage, but no major benefit has been found. Along the same lines, a study of the Japanese condiment wasabi, used to spice up sushi, did not find it was an effective decongestant either.

So go ahead and enjoy spicy foods if you like the taste and your stomach doesn't object, but I wouldn't count on them to have much long-lasting benefit on your sinus symptoms.

## Alcohol

It's not uncommon for people with sinusitis to develop a new infection or see their symptoms flare up within twenty-four hours of drinking an alcoholic beverage. The problem is not the alcohol itself but the presence of impurities known as congeners, which are the by-products of the fermentation and aging process. Congeners provide much of the beverage's taste and aroma, but some have histamine-like properties. Similar to what happens with an allergic reaction to pollen or dust, individuals who are sensitive to these impurities can experience nasal congestion, drainage, and headaches.

You may have this alcohol sensitivity without knowing it. If you suspect you might, you can usually sidestep this problem by avoiding alcoholic beverages likely to contain high amounts of congeners. If you like wine, you're better off with white wines, especially those processed in stainless steel containers, instead of red wines, which are aged in wooden barrels and contain many more by-products. If you drink liquor, you'll have fewer problems with clear varieties, such as vodka (especially brands that are "smoother" and have been highly distilled), than with darker, aged liquors, like bourbon and scotch. The amount of congeners in beer varies, but in general, lighter colored beers have fewer than darker ones.

And if you heed these instructions, the next morning you may notice a bonus benefit along with reduced sinus symptoms—it's actually the congeners, as much as the alcohol, that are believed to be the cause of a hangover.

## Smoking

In addition to damaging your lungs, cigarette smoking impairs the function of the tiny hairs (cilia) in your nasal passages and sinuses that sweep out mucus and debris. When cilia don't function well, mucus and bacteria build up in the sinuses, leading to infections. If you smoke, quitting is probably the single most important step you can take to improve your sinus symptoms. Cilia are resilient, so after you quit smoking, their normal function returns, which often leads to fewer sinus infections.

## The Workplace

The incidence of sinusitis and asthma has increased during the past decade. Although the cause for this increase remains unknown, one theory is that it's because more people are working in sealed buildings where they can't open a window to let in fresh air. Instead, the interior air is constantly recirculated. As a result, it tends to be quite dry. And if the building is contaminated with indoor pollutants—such as mold and spores, fibers from carpeting and upholstery, and chemicals in insulation and copy machines— then the ventilation system serves to recirculate the impurities. Tainted air can irritate the lining of your nose, lungs, and sinuses, blocking breathing and setting the stage for an infection. This reaction can be due to a true allergic response in which your body's immune system triggers the release of a host of inflammatory factors. It can also result from direct inflammation in which a chemical, for example, burns or irritates the nasal mucosa.

This phenomenon of contaminated workplaces is known as sick building syndrome. Its existence at a given site can be difficult to define and measure, but it's something to consider if any of the following are true:

- Your nasal and sinus symptoms are worse at work.
- Coworkers who sit near you come down with similar symptoms.
- You work in a particularly old building with poor ventilation.

If you suspect there's a problem, talk to your supervisor or building manager about what can be done to improve air quality. You can also contact the local representative of the Environmental Protection Agency. A link on the agency's website (epa.gov/

iaq/whereyoulive.html) includes helpful background and contact information.

Some of my patients who were convinced their repeated sinus infections were the result of workplace pollutants received dramatic improvement by simply moving their desks to a different location (such as away from an overhead vent). In other cases, a portable air filter at the desk provided relief. In the most severe cases, the only solution may be moving to a different building or finding a new job. I recognize it's a lot easier said than done, but sometimes radical changes in lifestyle and workplace may be called for when recurrent sinus infections are seriously affecting the quality of your life.

## The Fragrance Factor

Strong perfumes and colognes are another potential workplace hazard for people with sinusitis, especially in offices where everyone is crammed side by side into small cubicles. Such unintended sharing of personal air space can cause what might be called sick cubicle syndrome. If you have a particular sensitivity to strong fragrances, you might experience an eruption of nasal and sinus symptoms, including itchy eyes and nose, runny nose, and congestion, all of which can lead to a full-blown case of sinusitis.

Raising this issue without offending your coworker can be a touchy matter. But if you're tactful, you should find that the benefits to your health outweigh the temporary social discomfort. You might also discuss the problem with your boss if implementing an across-the-board policy seems like an easier path than taking it up with the pungent coworker. A growing number of workplaces (as well as schools and houses of worship) have enacted bans on colognes and fragrances.

## What's Next

Next, we'll take a look at some of the nontraditional therapies that may benefit people with sinusitis.

# CHAPTER 13

# Alternative Therapies for Sinusitis

People with sinusitis who don't get better with conventional therapy often try alternative treatments, such as acupuncture, herbs, vitamins, homeopathy, and more. If you're contemplating entering the world of alternative therapies, you're probably wondering, "Do they work?"

This is a tricky question to answer. Unfortunately, few rigorous studies have examined whether alternative therapies actually benefit people with sinusitis (or other chronic diseases, for that matter). Alternative therapies are not strictly regulated by the federal government, so practitioners and manufacturers have little incentive to conduct costly studies proving their techniques and products are safe and effective. Without research, we're left with anecdotal evidence, which makes it hard for me as a physician to give a ringing endorsement of any particular alternative therapy.

That does not mean I oppose alternative therapies. There is much that modern medicine does not understand and cannot account for, so I don't discourage anyone from trying something that might relieve symptoms, so long as it won't make things worse.

It's worth noting that many of today's accepted treatments are derived from plants and at one time would have been considered alternative. For example, digitalis, a drug used to treat heart disease, is made from the leaves of the foxglove plant. In the sinus arena, the widely used mucus-thinning agent guaifenesin was developed from the resin of guaiac wood. So what's considered alternative today may one day become a mainstay of conventional treatment.

## Using Common Sense

When patients ask me about trying an alternative therapy, I encourage them to give it a try with three caveats:

- Make sure the treatment is not potentially dangerous. The majority of alternative treatments are not, but reports of problems occasionally surface, such as those that led the FDA to ban sales of dietary supplements containing the herb ephedra in 2003.
- Alternative therapies should be used in conjunction with established treatments, not in place of them. If your doctor gives you a four-week prescription of an antibiotic, do not stop taking it halfway through because you've decided to try an herbal supplement or vitamin.
- Let your doctor know if you're using an alternative therapy. This is most crucial with herbs but is a good idea in general, in case the alternative treatment is known to diminish or otherwise affect the conventional therapy you're receiving.

Following is a rundown of the alternative treatments most often used by people with sinusitis.

## Acupuncture

This centuries-old Chinese practice is based on the theory that your physical and mental health depends on a natural flow of energy called qi (pronounced "chee"), which courses along fourteen pathways known as meridians. When this flow becomes blocked, disease and pain—including sinusitis and sinus pain—develop. Acupuncture is intended to relieve this blockage and provide relief.

An acupuncturist inserts fine, sterile needles through the skin along the various meridians. Certain points, particularly those at the side of the nose and in the web of the hand between the thumb and index finger, are thought to be most effective in treating sinus disease.

Many of my patients who have tried acupuncture report that it does indeed help relieve the headache and pain associated with sinusitis when medications haven't worked. A much smaller percentage have found it improves congestion and drainage.

Acupressure is based on the same principle as acupuncture, but direct finger pressure is used to stimulate the meridian points instead of needles.

## Herbal Therapy

Herbs have been and remain the mainstay of indigenous healing practices throughout much of the world. In the United States, herbal supplements are the leading form of alternative health therapy, and their use drives a multibillion-dollar industry.

Even so, FDA regulation of herbs remains limited. According to the 1994 Dietary Supplement Health and Education Act, herbs do not require FDA review. As long as the label does not make unsupported scientific claims, manufacturers have much leeway in promoting the alleged benefits of their products. The FDA must prove an herb unsafe to remove it from the market.

So consumers need to exercise care when making a purchase. Because supplements' ingredients and purity can vary greatly among manufacturers, it's best to buy products that say "standardized extracts" on the label. Note that a supplement's effectiveness may vary from brand to brand, even if the dosage is the same. That's because differing crops and processing methods yield varying strength and purity. A good analogy is the different taste and qualities of wines. Despite starting with the same grapes, different vineyards end up producing very different bottles of wine.

Among the herbs most frequently claimed to alleviate sinus symptoms are the following:

- **Echinacea.** Thought to enhance the immune system and help prevent infections, this popular herb is used widely to reduce the symptoms and duration of colds and flulike illnesses. Laboratory studies have suggested that it enhances the body's replication of T cells, white blood cells used to fight infection. Clinical trials looking at the efficacy of echinacea for infections have yielded mixed results.
- **Goldenseal.** Referred to as nature's antibiotic because of its presumed antibacterial and anti-inflammatory properties, this herb was introduced to early settlers by Cherokee Indians, who used it as a wash for skin diseases and wounds. After the Civil War, it became an ingredient in many patent medicines, and today its adherents use it to treat everything from sore throats to canker sores to premenstrual syndrome. Goldenseal's benefits are often attributed to berberine, an active ingredient.
- **Bromelain.** Thought to reduce inflammation, bromelain is a compound present in pineapples. Three studies performed in the 1960s showed that patients who took bromelain tablets with an antibiotic reported greater sinusitis symptom relief (reduced nasal inflammation, mucus discharge, and congestion) than people who took the antibiotic alone.

If you take herbs to ease sinus symptoms or with other goals in mind (increased energy, enhanced memory, and so on), I want to stress the importance of keeping your doctor posted, for two reasons. First, like conventional medications, herbs often have side effects. They can affect preexisting health conditions, including hypertension and diabetes, and interact with medications you may be taking. Second, herbs can increase bleeding during surgery, so it's crucial that your doctor know what you're taking if you're planning sinus surgery (or any type of surgery, for that matter). Be especially aware of the Four Gs—garlic, ginger, ginkgo, and ginseng—all of which are known to increase bleeding. Ginseng, for example, inhibits the function of platelets, a blood component required for clotting. I advise my patients to stop taking these herbs at least two weeks before sinus surgery.

For detailed, objective information on herbal supplements, I recommend looking at the website run by the American Herbal Products Association (ahpa.org).

## Nutritional Supplements

Vitamin C and zinc are the two supplements most often claimed to prevent infections. Research in this area has focused on colds; whether these products have any beneficial effect on sinusitis—in terms of either warding off infections or shortening their duration—is not known.

In the 1970s, Nobel Prize–winning chemist Linus Pauling became a vocal advocate for taking large doses of vitamin C at the first signs of a cold. Despite his claims, controlled studies failed to show any effect of this vitamin on decreasing the severity or duration of cold symptoms.

There is, however, some evidence to supports zinc's infection-fighting properties. Zicam, a zinc-containing nasal gel, has been shown to reduce a cold's duration if you start using it within the first twenty-four hours of the onset of symptoms. The drawback of this over-the-counter preparation is that it must be sprayed into the nose every four hours for one to two weeks to be effective. Zinc is also available in lozenge form, as the product Cold-Eze, but the use of this oral preparation for reducing colds has yielded mixed results.

## Homeopathic Medicine

Devised more than two hundred years ago by the German physician Samuel Hahnemann, homeopathy is based on the principle of "Like cures like." In other words, the same substance that in large doses causes a symptom will in small doses alleviate that symptom.

People who go to homeopathic doctors typically receive a highly diluted medicine (or medicine combination) designed to alleviate their symptoms. A number of homeopathic sinus remedies are available over the counter, including the nasal spray Sinu-Free and the zinc-based Zicam (mentioned earlier). The modern practice of homeopathy in the United States is regulated, and homeopathic medicines must be approved by the FDA.

## Stress Reduction Techniques

In case you haven't noticed, we live in an increasingly stressful world. Chronic illnesses in general, and sinus symptoms in particular, tend to worsen during times of emotional and physical stress. Who can argue with the concept of stress reduction?

The challenge is to find something you enjoy doing each day that can temporarily remove you from the world of cell phones, computers, carpools, and coworkers. In 1975 Dr. Herbert Benson of Harvard Medical School authored *The Relaxation Response*, which described a simple breathing exercise for mind-body relaxation. The book became a bestseller, and Benson's method continues to help stressed-out people today.

Others find relaxation through different channels, such as yoga, tai chi, meditation, and biofeedback. Regular exercise (for example, jogging, working out at the gym, or swimming laps in a pool) is also an effective stress reliever. Whatever your source of relaxation, it must be something you enjoy doing, not a chore, so that you'll be able to stick with it for the long haul and reap the physical and mental health benefits.

## What's Next

What do you do when none of the conventional and alternative treatments we've discussed offer symptom relief? For some people—perhaps one in five—surgery is a viable option. In the next chapter, we'll look at the factors that can help you decide whether you would make a good surgical candidate.

# Surgery for Sinusitis

# 14

# Making the Decision to Have Sinus Surgery

So you've tried just about every sinus medication, including repeated courses of antibiotics, and you're still no better. Now what?

For some people, an operation to open and drain blocked sinuses can have a dramatic effect. But how do you know if you're a good candidate for surgery? Because sinusitis is not a life-threatening condition, deciding whether to have surgery is not black and white but, rather, shades of gray. Let's look at some of the issues that arise as you and your doctor make this important decision.

## Your Doctor's Recommendation

Your ENT doctor bases his recommendation on your history, endoscopic exam, and CT scan findings. (I'll use the terms ENT doctor and surgeon interchangeably because it's the ENT doctor who performs the surgery.) A key issue is the number of annual infections. As a rule of thumb, it's time to consider surgery if you have four or more sinus infections each year. If this is the case, you're spending a large percentage of your time suffering and recovering from infections, so surgery's benefits are likely to be tangible.

Another consideration is the duration of your infections. Over time, some people find that infections that formerly lasted a few days are now lasting several weeks because antibiotics are less effective. Surgery may still be advisable for someone who has only two or three infections a year if they last several weeks or months.

Older people often wonder if their age should be a factor in deciding whether to have sinus surgery. As long as you're otherwise healthy, advancing age should not discourage you from surgery. I've operated on many people in their eighties with positive results.

## It's Your Decision

If your doctor advises that you are likely to benefit from surgery, then you need to think about whether surgery's potential benefits outweigh its discomforts and risks.

Here, the key issue is quality of life. Think about how sinusitis affects your day-to-day ability to function. How many sick days from work do you take? Does sinusitis affect your social life? Are you often tired? How do you feel about the amount of medication you take? Would your enjoyment of life change appreciably if you had fewer infections?

It's a very personal decision. One individual may find that missing two to three weeks of work each year for sickness is acceptable, while another feels it prevents him or her from reaching important career goals. The more you feel sinusitis is affecting your quality of life, the more the pendulum swings in favor of surgery.

## Realistic Expectations

It's important to have realistic expectations of what the procedure is likely to accomplish. Bear in mind that for most patients, sinus surgery does not provide a complete cure. Some sinus infections will still occur, but the frequency and severity of infections will be reduced. If you've had five or six sinus infections each year, surgery often can reduce the number to two or three. Not every cold will turn into another case of sinusitis. And if the procedure is successful, infections that do occur will be of shorter duration; a briefer course of antibiotics will control your symptoms.

You should also be aware that surgery will not eliminate the underlying cause of your sinus problems. If you have allergies, surgery does not cure them, so symptoms such as itchy eyes, sneezing, and thin postnasal drip are likely to remain, along with the need for allergy medications. And while surgeons can remove polyps, they can't eliminate the problem that causes them to grow. So individuals with large polyps are likely to need additional surgery when polyps regrow.

One thing that's hard to predict is whether patients whose sense of smell has been impaired by sinusitis will regain this function. It depends on the cause of the defect. If repeated infections and polyp growth have severely eroded the nerve endings on olfactory receptors, then smell is not likely to return after surgery. If, on the other hand, loss of smell is caused by polyps and swollen tissue that block odor molecules in the air from reaching the smell receptors in the back of the nose, then removing the polyps and obstructions should lead to a return in smell.

In terms of the Sinusitis Spectrum (see Figure 14.1), Locals whose CT scans show limited obstruction of the sinuses usually respond well to surgery because the anatomical cause of obstruction often can be permanently eliminated. In many cases, normal sinus function is restored. Systemics whose sinusitis is caused by polyps or extensive mucosal swelling can expect improvement, although without a complete cure. The nose and sinuses will be more open, but underlying inflammation of the mucous membranes lining these passages will remain. The long-term success of sinus surgery for Intermediates varies, depending on whether the severity of their disease places them closer on the Sinusitis Spectrum to Locals or Systemics.

**FIGURE 14.1** The Sinusitis Spectrum—Surgery

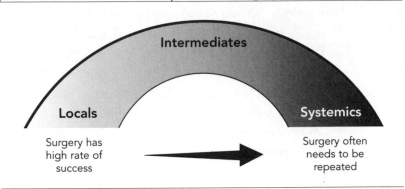

The likelihood that surgery will be curative or will need to be repeated corresponds to the location of one's disease along the Sinusitis Spectrum.

## Surgery Really Does Help

Although it's important to have realistic expectations, I don't mean to downplay surgery's genuine benefits. Two studies I conducted with Dr. Richard Gliklich and my colleagues at Harvard University offer insight into how surgery affects people's lives.

The first study, published in 1997, followed more than one hundred patients who underwent surgery for chronic sinusitis. They rated their symptoms (such as headache, congestion, and drainage) before surgery and afterward at regular intervals for one year. They also reported on use of sinus medications and completed questionnaires about how sinusitis affected their quality of life. Overall, 82 percent of patients were found to have significant improvement following sinus surgery.

The second study, published a year later, focused exclusively on the economics of sinus surgery. We found that the cost of sinus medications—including prescription and over-the-counter remedies—averaged $1,220 per patient per year before surgery and $629 after surgery, a 48 percent reduction.

Because surgical techniques have continued to improve in the past decade and more sinus medications are now available, I suspect that both the 82 percent symptom improvement rate and the 48 percent reduction in medication costs would be even greater if we conducted similar studies today.

## Factoring in Complications

An additional factor to consider when contemplating sinus surgery is the risk of complications. Although technological advances have reduced the incidence of surgical complications, the element of risk can never be completely eliminated. Here's a list of complications associated with sinus surgery, starting with the most common:

- **Bleeding.** The nose and sinuses are prone to bleeding during and after surgery because they have a rich blood supply. If bleeding does occur, it can usually be controlled by nasal packing. I'll discuss postsurgical bleeding in Chapter 16.
- **Infection.** Bacteria can multiply on the raw tissue and crusts that are present in the nose after surgery, leading to a sinus infection. A doctor can treat such infections with an antibiotic and by cleaning out the nose.

Bleeding and infection each occur in about 5 percent of patients. Some rarer complications include:

- **Impaired breathing.** Temporary nasal congestion from swelling is expected after surgery. Long-term nasal airway obstruction may occur if dense scar tissue forms after surgery and blocks the nasal passages.
- **Loss of smell.** Many patients have a decreased sense of smell for a week or two following surgery because of swollen nasal membranes. Long-term impairment may result if the region of the olfactory nerve is inadvertently damaged during surgery or if dense scar tissue forms and blocks odor molecules from reaching smell receptors in the nose.

- **Excessive tearing.** The duct that drains tears from the eye into the nose runs through the wall of the maxillary sinus. If this duct is injured during surgery, excessive tearing may result, requiring additional surgery to restore proper tear drainage.

Very rare but serious complications include the following:

- **Spinal fluid leak.** If the layer of bone separating the sinuses from the brain is breached during surgery, the clear cerebral spinal fluid (CSF) that surrounds the brain can leak into the nose. If this leak persists, the patient risks developing meningitis, which can be life-threatening. A CSF leak can be closed immediately if it's recognized during surgery. If it's not, additional endoscopic surgery to close the leak will likely be needed. Such corrective surgery is generally performed through the nostril and involves placing a tissue patch over the leakage site.
- **Decreased vision.** Injury to the eye itself or the surrounding muscles and nerves may leave patients with impaired vision, including double vision or blindness.
- **Stroke.** The carotid arteries run through the walls of the sphenoid sinuses. If one is injured during surgery, blood flow to the brain may be interrupted, resulting in a stroke.

Although these last complications sound frightening, it's important to realize that they are extremely rare. Your doctor will review all potential complications that apply to your surgery and answer any questions you may have.

## What's Next

Deciding whether you're a good candidate for surgery is an important first step. Now, let's look at what sinus surgery entails.

# CHAPTER 15

# What to Expect with Sinus Surgery

Today's sinus surgery bears little resemblance to what it was twenty-five years ago. Let's take a look at some of the major developments that have made the surgical experience less painful for patients and improved the likelihood of postoperative success.

## A Brief History of Sinus Surgery

During the first half of the twentieth century, surgeons were hindered by their limited understanding of sinus function, as well as a lack of easy access to the sinuses and nasal passages. They tended to go directly where the pain was; if a patient's maxillary sinus kept getting infected, then the inside of that sinus was the focus of the operation. The surgeon made incisions in the gum of the patient's upper jaw, scraped out the inflamed sinus lining, and created an artificial passageway for mucus to drain into the nose. This surgery, which was commonly performed until the 1980s, is known as a Caldwell-Luc procedure.

For patients with diseased frontal or ethmoid sinuses, surgery often required a facial incision—either just above the eye or alongside the nose—that left a scar. Again, the surgeon opened up the sinus and scraped out the lining.

In some cases, the surgeon could operate exclusively through the nose, using a speculum to spread the nostrils and a bright headlight to see inside the nasal cavities. However, visibility was limited, and it was often a challenge to see and access the depths of the sinuses.

To prevent postoperative bleeding, the inside of the nose had to be packed with long strips of gauze. This packing often stayed in for a week, during which patients could breathe only through their mouths. And the trauma of the surgery left patients bruised and swollen.

While these procedures worked for some people, many saw little or no improvement. Why? One problem was poor visualization—surgeons had difficulty distinguishing between diseased and healthy tissue. Another was a lack of understanding of the sinus drainage pathways through the ostiomeatal complex (OMC), the series of narrow channels and openings that serves as a common drainage pathway for the ethmoid, maxillary, and frontal sinuses. As a result, surgeons often did too much or too little surgery—or both. Diseased tissue in the OMC region was frequently left behind, so the sinuses eventually became obstructed again. And too much normal tissue (such as healthy bone, cartilage, and mucous membranes) was removed, which resulted in the formation of scar tissue and poor sinus function.

## The Modern Way: Minimally Invasive Surgery

In the 1980s a revolution took place in sinus surgery that led to the development of functional endoscopic sinus surgery, or FESS for short. (Nowadays, many ENT doctors drop the "functional" and simply call it ESS.) The advantage of ESS is that it's much less traumatic on the body than older techniques. Patients are no longer left black and blue, and they often don't need nasal packing. Those who do can almost always have it removed the following day.

The development of ESS was made possible by the nexus of three separate advances: nasal endoscopes, sinus CT scans, and the concept of the OMC.

The invention of nasal endoscopes gave surgeons a new technique for accessing the sinuses. These thin telescopes with high-resolution optics allowed for excellent visualization deep within the nose. Instead of cutting through the gums or on the face, surgeons could now enter through the nostrils and get a bright, magnified view inside the sinus cavities.

The 1980s also witnessed a move from plain x-rays to CT scans for evaluating sinus anatomy. For the first time, surgeons could see a picture of the OMC in vivid detail and identify localized obstructions. This enabled them to do a much better job of evaluating whether surgery was likely to benefit a particular patient. And if it was, they knew more precisely what needed to be done.

Around the same time that nasal endoscopes and sinus CT scans were introduced, an Austrian ENT doctor named Walter Messerklinger proposed a novel idea regarding the cause of sinusitis and its surgical treatment. According to Messerklinger, frontal and maxillary sinus infections were actually *secondary* obstructions. The *primary* cause of sinus obstruction lay in the OMC region of the ethmoid sinuses. Open up the ethmoids, he said, and the maxillary and frontal sinuses (which drain through the ethmoids) will resume normal function. There was no need to create artificial passageways or to scrape the interior sinus lining.

Messerklinger's theory was appealing because it meant less extensive surgery could be performed and recovery could be swifter. It was also inviting philosophically, since it meant the final result would more closely approximate natural sinus function.

But would it work? I remember when Dr. Heinz Stammberger, a pupil of Dr. Messerklinger's, first promoted this new concept to American surgeons at a medical conference in 1985. Many of us in the audience were skeptical. But after practicing the surgery in the laboratory and then performing it on selected patients, we became believers. As the technique was refined, results continued to improve. By the mid-1990s, ESS was used for the majority of sinus surgeries, and it remains the standard of care today.

Now let's look at the steps of basic sinus surgery, starting with anesthesia.

## Anesthesia

ESS can be performed under either local or general anesthesia. The choice depends on the patient, surgeon, and procedure performed.

Local anesthesia is administered by injections to the nose, and you receive supplemental sedation through an IV line in your arm. You may drift in and out of consciousness during the surgery.

For general anesthesia, you're put to sleep with medication administered through the IV line, and you're kept asleep with a gas you inhale through a tube in your mouth. You have no awareness at all.

Your surgeon may prefer one type of anesthesia or the other. I perform most of my surgeries with patients under general anesthesia, which I find is easier on both the patient and the surgeon.

Refinements in technology have made the risk of anesthesia complications extremely low, but it is possible to have an adverse reaction. You'll have an opportunity to talk with the anesthesiologist before surgery to discuss any concerns you may have.

## The Preoperative Visit

Sometime prior to your surgery, you'll meet with your ENT doctor to review the details of surgery and sign surgical consent forms. The preoperative visit is a good time to let him know about any recent changes in your overall health. It will also give you an opportunity to ask any remaining questions you might have about your surgery. You may want to prepare a written list of questions so you won't forget to ask something important.

If you're in the midst of a sinus infection, your doctor may prescribe an antibiotic to clear the infection before surgery. Patients are usually advised to stop taking aspirin and aspirin-containing products one to two weeks prior to surgery; aspirin thins the blood and increases the risk of bleeding during surgery.

You also should not take products containing ibuprofen (such as Advil and Motrin) or other nonsteroidal anti-inflammatory agents within forty-eight hours of surgery.

## Arriving for Surgery

When you arrive at the hospital, a nurse will check you in, review your medical history (including drug allergies), and take your vital signs. You'll also have a chance to meet the anesthesiologist, if you haven't already done so. The surgeon may be there as well; if so, you can ask any last-minute questions you may have.

When it's time for surgery, you'll lie down on a stretcher and be wheeled into the operating room. Sinus surgery typically requires a minimum of four people: a surgeon, an anesthesiologist, and two nurses. The anesthesiologist will monitor your vital signs, such as heart rate, blood pressure, and oxygen level in your blood. The scrub nurse hands instruments to the surgeon. The circulating nurse positions you, sets up the equipment, and gets any additional items the surgeon might ask for during the procedure.

Once the anesthesia has been administered, the actual surgery begins. It typically lasts from one to two hours.

## The Operation

During endoscopic sinus surgery, the surgeon uses one hand to insert the endoscope into the nose and the other hand to pass a variety of specialized instruments (such as tiny scalpels, curettes, forceps, and a suction device to remove blood and mucus) alongside the endoscope.

For basic ESS, the surgeon proceeds through the following steps:

1. Open the OMC to reveal the site of maxillary sinus drainage.
2. Clear and enlarge the maxillary ostium by removing obstructing tissue, including swollen mucous membranes and polyps.

3. Open the front of the ethmoid sinus (anterior ethmoid air cells).

4. Remove the thin bony partitions and swollen membranes within the honeycomb-like air cells of the anterior ethmoid sinus.

5. If disease extends into the back of the ethmoid sinus (posterior air cells), open and remove diseased tissue in this region as well.

During ESS, the surgeon's goal is to remove any diseased tissue obstructing the sinuses and causing infections. Ideally, elimination of this obstructing tissue will allow the formerly blocked sinus passages to remain open permanently (see Figure 15.1).

At the same time, the surgeon attempts to avoid removing normal tissue or mildly diseased tissue that is likely to return to normal once the infected sinus has healed (see the sidebar "Small-Hole Technique"). The more tissue that is removed, the longer it takes to recover and the greater the risk of complications. Deciding what tissue to remove and what to leave behind is often a judgment call. The principle I like to follow is "Do as little as possible but as much as necessary."

Samples of tissue removed during surgery are routinely sent to a lab for analysis. In the unlikely event that you have a benign or malignant tumor, it would show up during this analysis. I'll discuss sinus tumors in greater detail in Chapter 18.

Once the surgery is over, the surgeon decides whether to pack your nose, based on the likelihood of postoperative bleeding. He can use a soft biodegradable substance (which slowly dissolves) or a spongelike material (which is removed later that day or the next morning).

## Specialized Instruments

Today's surgeons have access to a variety of additional tools in the operating room. Whether or not a surgeon uses these devices is a

FIGURE 15.1 Sinuses Before and After Surgery

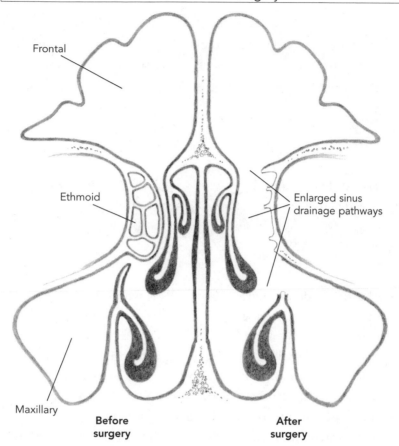

Frontal

Ethmoid

Enlarged sinus
drainage pathways

Maxillary

**Before
surgery**

**After
surgery**

*The left side of the diagram shows normal sinus anatomy. The right side shows what things look like after surgery to enlarge the sinus ostia and enhance drainage of the frontal, ethmoid, and maxillary sinuses. Note that removal of the honeycomb-like ethmoid sinuses leaves a much larger passageway through which mucus can now drain.*

matter of personal preference—it's possible to do effective sinus surgery with or without them.

- **Video cameras.** Although the surgeon can perform the operation by looking directly through the eyepiece of the endoscope, nowadays most surgeons operate with the help

## Small-Hole Technique

Some surgeons favor what's called the small-hole technique (also known as MIST, for minimally invasive surgical technique), which involves opening the ethmoid sinus but leaving alone the maxillary sinus ostia and most surrounding tissue. The hope is that remaining swollen tissue will return to normal and the patient will have a quicker recovery.

Not enough research has been done to know whether the small-hole technique is better than, worse than, or the same as standard ESS. For now, I believe it's acceptable for patients with limited disease, but it probably is less successful than ESS for those with moderate to advanced disease.

of a tiny video camera. This camera, which is attached to the endoscope's eyepiece, displays a magnified image of the nasal interior on a video monitor. The surgeon performs the operation while looking at the monitor.

- **Microdebriders.** A microdebrider (also known as a microdissector or shaver) is a thin hollow tube with a rotating blade at one end and a suction device at the other. The surgeon activates the blade with a foot pedal and shaves away tissue, which automatically gets suctioned down the tube. Such motorized instrumentation was first used by orthopedic surgeons to shave cartilage during knee surgery. Microdebriders were adapted for sinus surgery because of the efficient manner in which they remove polyps and swollen membranes. Some surgeons use microdebriders for all their sinus surgeries. I prefer to use them for selected cases, such as for patients who have large polyps.
- **Lasers.** Lasers use an intensively focused beam of light to vaporize tissue and simultaneously seal blood vessels—a combination that makes them ideal for surgeries requiring precise tissue removal. When ESS was first introduced, many surgeons used lasers to perform the procedure.

However, because lasers remove tissue by burning rather than cutting, patients who underwent laser ESS were found to have more swelling and congestion during the postoperative healing period. As a result, lasers are now used infrequently for sinus surgery. Nevertheless, they remain an effective tool for bloodless removal of swollen tissue, particularly in patients who have enlarged turbinates.

## Advanced Techniques

As has been noted, most sinus surgeries center on the OMC and the maxillary and ethmoid sinuses. However, in patients with frequent infections of the frontal or sphenoid sinuses, it may be necessary to do more extensive surgery. Not all ENT doctors perform the more advanced techniques, so patients who need one of the following procedures may be referred to a surgeon specializing in difficult cases.

- **Sphenoid sinusotomy.** If an infected sphenoid sinus doesn't clear with medications, a surgeon can choose to enlarge the sphenoid ostia and drain entrapped fluid. Because of the sphenoid's sensitive location near the optic nerve and brain, this surgery can be delicate. Nevertheless, when properly performed, it is a safe and effective way to treat sphenoid sinusitis.
- **Frontal sinusotomy.** Here, the surgeon uses endoscopic instruments through the nose to open and enlarge the frontal sinus ostia. The frontal sinuses are more difficult to reach because of their location high up in the forehead. Surgeons must use longer, curved instruments and endoscopes with angled views. Although a frontal sinusotomy is more complex than standard surgery, it is usually successful at relieving frontal headaches.
- **Frontal sinus drillout.** If a frontal sinusotomy doesn't work—or if the surgeon suspects it won't—another option is to remove the entire bony floor of the frontal sinus with

139

a drill passed alongside the endoscope. This surgery, also known as a Modified Lothrop procedure or a Draf 3 operation, creates a very large opening between the frontal sinus and nose, maximizing mucus drainage. It takes longer to perform than normal sinus surgery, and healing can also take more time, because of the amount of bone removed.

• **Frontal sinus obliteration.** An alternative treatment for frontal sinusitis is elimination of the frontal sinuses altogether. As you may recall from Chapter 2, some people never develop frontal sinuses, and they get along just fine. Frontal sinus obliteration is performed through an incision in the scalp or forehead. The surgeon makes an opening through the bony sinus wall, removes all the tissue inside with a drill, fills up the empty sinus with a piece of fat taken from the abdomen, and then reseals the sinus. When healing is finished, fat cells completely fill the sinus, and there is no longer any air-containing sinus cavity to become infected. Although frontal sinus obliteration is much more invasive than conventional endoscopic sinus surgery, it has been performed for more than thirty years and has a long-term success rate of more than 90 percent.

Recently, I have begun performing frontal sinus obliteration with an endoscope and drill passed into the frontal sinus through a small incision in the eyebrow. This minimally invasive approach may prove useful for selected patients with small- or medium-sized frontal sinuses, but the long-term success rate is not yet known.

## Image-Guided Surgery

Image-guided surgery is a recent development that you may benefit from, particularly if you have an advanced procedure. Here, the same Global Positioning technology that directs drivers to their destinations and missiles to their targets is used to help surgeons guide their instruments through the sinus cavities with millimeter accuracy.

Image-guidance systems enable a surgeon to monitor the precise location of his instruments within the sinus cavities throughout surgery. These systems use either an infrared beam or an electromagnetic signal to track the position of the instruments relative to the patient's head. They require the patient to wear a special headset during surgery. (For some image-guidance systems, the same headset is worn by the patient during the preoperative sinus CT scan.) The location of the tip of the instruments is depicted by crosshairs on a three-dimensional video display of the patient's sinus CT scan, as shown in Figures 15.2 and 15.3.

Image-guided surgery's advantage is that it reduces the element of guesswork—the surgeon always knows exactly where he is. For this reason, it's most helpful in difficult cases. During a study of one thousand image-guided sinus surgeries, I surveyed forty-two

**FIGURE 15.2** Image-Guided Surgery

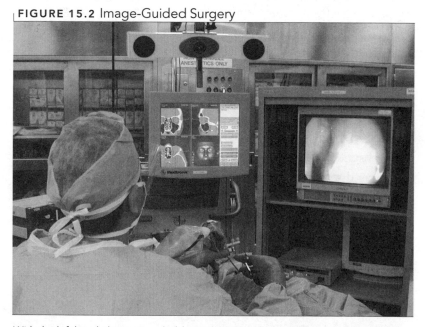

*With the left hand, the surgeon holds a video camera attached to an endoscope that displays a magnified view of the nasal cavity on the video monitor (right). With the other hand, he passes instruments alongside the endoscope to remove diseased tissue. The image-guidance system uses an infrared camera (horizontal white bar at top) to monitor the location of the tip of the surgical instrument, which is displayed on a second video monitor (center).*

**FIGURE 15.3** Video Display During Image-Guided Surgery

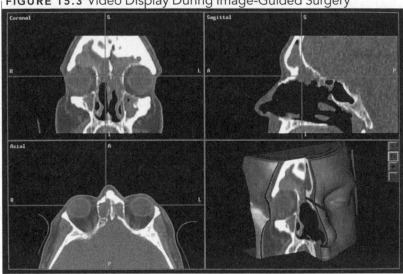

*The video display of an image-guidance system during sinus surgery shows the location of a surgical instrument depicted by crosshairs on three different views of the patient's CT scan. The lower-right quadrant shows a three-dimensional reconstruction of the patient's sinus anatomy, with the tip of the surgical instrument (depicted as a black pointer) in the ethmoid sinus.*

surgeons who used this new technology at the Massachusetts Eye and Ear Infirmary from 1996 to 2002. They found it to be particularly helpful in cases where the normal surgical landmarks were absent, a common occurrence among patients who have extensive disease or who have undergone previous surgery.

Although image-guidance systems have the potential to enhance surgery's safety and efficacy, they also have drawbacks. Like any fancy new computer, they take time to master, and bugs in the system sometimes arise. Also, these systems add time and expense to the operation, so they are not meant to be used for routine sinus surgery.

## What's Next

Now that you know what surgery involves, let's examine what you can expect in the days, weeks, and months afterward.

# CHAPTER 16

# Recovering from Sinus Surgery

Now that surgery is over, you can look forward to better breathing and fewer sinus infections. But before you get there, the healing process must run its course. Recovery from sinus surgery tends to vary according to the patient and the extent of the operation. For most people, it's a slow but steady journey in which you feel a little better each day and gradually ease back into your normal routine over several weeks. Following is an overview of what you can expect.

## Going Home: The First Few Days

In the days immediately following sinus surgery, you're likely to experience a few common postoperative symptoms:

- **Fatigue.** For the first week, you'll feel more tired than usual. Don't be surprised if you nap during the day and need more sleep than normal at night, especially for the first few days. Don't fight it—it's all part of the healing process.

    The fatigue from sinus surgery can be deceptive; unlike most other types of surgery, you don't bear external scars as a reminder of what you've been through. But your body still needs time to recover. Early on, calories that would normally be available for physical activity are instead directed toward healing your nasal and sinus passages.

- **Dull headache.** After surgery, you'll probably have a headache for a day or two, but it should improve as the week progresses. Don't hesitate to take prescribed pain medication, especially at night, when headaches tend to be worse. Sleeping with your head elevated on several pillows can also help.

- **Bloody mucus drainage.** You can expect some mucus mixed with blood to drain from your nose for up to one week. This drainage will be greatest the first two days, during which you may want to tape a gauze bandage beneath your nose.

- **Nasal congestion.** You'll probably find that you can't breathe very well through your nose right after surgery because of swelling and bloody mucus drainage. For the first three days, you should avoid blowing your nose, as this may cause bleeding. From then on, you may blow your nose gently if necessary.

    The best way to clear your nose of mucus, as well as bits of dried blood that may accumulate, is with saline irrigation. I can't overemphasize how critical postsurgical irrigation is; if you're not already familiar with the technique, you may wish to refer to the instructions in Chapter 7. You should start irrigating the day after surgery and do it twice a day for at least a week. Within a week, you should be able to move air in and out of your nose fairly well, although there will still be some restriction. Be patient. In two to three weeks, you should be breathing better than ever.

## What to Watch Out For

Fatigue, headache, blood-tinged mucus, and congestion are all normal postoperative symptoms that should not raise any red flags.

However, two other postoperative symptoms—bleeding and fever—do warrant concern.

- **Bleeding.** Continuous flow of bright red blood from the front of the nose that doesn't stop after a few minutes of sitting up and squeezing your nostrils together suggests a blood vessel has opened and won't shut. Such bleeding is most likely to occur in the first twenty-four hours after surgery but may occur anytime during the first week.

   If this sort of bleeding occurs, call your doctor or go to an emergency room, where a physician will cauterize or pack the nose to stop the bleeding. In rare cases, further surgery may be needed.
- **Infection.** Your doctor will prescribe an antibiotic for you to take after surgery. Even so, you're still at an above-average risk for infection because your immune system is not yet at full strength and the mucous membranes that ordinarily serve as a barrier to bacteria are still recovering.

   Also, *Staph aureus*, the bacteria that often reside in the nasal cavity, can multiply on the scablike crusts that form inside the nose after surgery. That's another reason why flushing out the crusts with saline irrigation is so important.

   Signs of infection include a fever of greater than 101 degrees, green nasal drainage, and severe facial pain or headache that's not relieved by medication. If any of these symptoms occur, you should call or see your doctor.

## Getting Back to Your Normal Self: The First Few Weeks

Here's what to expect in terms of everyday living:

- **Physical exercise.** You should avoid heavy lifting, straining, and exercise that might cause a nosebleed during the first week after surgery. Try not to do anything that causes blood to rush quickly to your head. For example, if you have to pick something up from the ground, bend at the knees to keep your head above your heart instead of bending at the waist. Also, parents need to be careful about picking up their young children.

After the first week, you may gradually resume normal activity if you feel up to it. Just use common sense. For exercise, slowly work your way up from brisk walking to running, and save backflips on the trampoline for last.

- **Work.** No matter your occupation, when you first start working again, you're likely to find that you tire more quickly than you'd expect for the first few days, so you may want to return to a lighter schedule than usual.

   How quickly you return to work depends on the nature of your job. If you work at a desk, you may be able to go back after a few days, although many people prefer to take a full week off so they return feeling good. If your job requires a lot of activity, you should definitely take a full week off. And if it involves heavy physical labor, I'd advise taking ten to fourteen days off so there's no further risk of bleeding by the time you return.

- **Eating and drinking.** You can eat and drink whatever you like after surgery. Be sure to take in plenty of fluids so you don't get dehydrated and your nasal secretions stay moist.

- **Driving.** You can resume driving two or three days after surgery if you feel that you can do so safely. Of course, don't drive if you're taking any narcotic pain medication.

- **Airplane travel.** Airplane travel is safe two weeks after sinus surgery as long as you haven't had complications. If you fly within a month of surgery and have residual nasal congestion or a history of ear pain with flying, you might want to take a bottle of nasal decongestant spray, like Afrin or Neo-Synephrine, with you on the plane. A couple of sprays in each nostril when you board and again at the start of descent should help keep your nose and ears open.

## Seeing Your ENT Doctor After Surgery

The first postoperative visit usually occurs about a week after surgery. Your surgeon will spray the inside of your nose with an anesthetic and then use an endoscope and a small forceps to remove any crusts that haven't already been flushed out with your daily saline irrigations. It's mildly uncomfortable but usually not painful.

Once the crusts are out, you should be able to breathe better. Any residual headache or facial pressure you've been having will likely improve within the next forty-eight hours, now that your sinuses are open and can drain again.

Additional follow-up visits will depend on the specifics of your surgery and how you're feeling. In some cases, you may need to return in another week or two for additional cleaning.

## Restarting Your Medications

If you regularly took allergy medications like nasal steroid sprays or antihistamines before the surgery, you can resume taking them within a week or two of surgery. Although surgery does not cure the underlying allergies, many patients find that their need for sinus and allergy medicines is much less following sinus surgery. Also, people with nasal polyps will want to resume regular use of nasal steroid sprays, because they are effective at slowing the regrowth of polyps.

## Completion of Healing: The First Few Months

After a month, most of the swelling in your nose should be gone and you should be feeling much better. However, your body is still not finished healing internally. It takes about eight to twelve weeks for the mucous membranes that line the nose and sinuses to fully recover and for sinus function to return to normal.

Many of my patients tell me that they don't feel the full benefits of surgery for several months. It may take until the next allergy season before people realize how much better they're breathing when the flowers are in bloom. Or it may be the next winter, when they notice that they're having fewer colds and infections than usual. Whatever the case, with time and patience, most people ultimately realize a tangible improvement from sinus surgery.

## Revision Surgery

For the majority of people who undergo sinus surgery, it's a one-time event. Others, however, need to return for one or more additional operations, a practice known as revision surgery.

Revision surgery is rare for Locals; it's needed in less than 5 percent of cases. The most common scenario is when a band of scar tissue forms and blocks the OMC or sinus ostia, a process known as fibrosis. A surgeon can usually fix the problem by cutting the scar band under either local or general anesthesia.

The rate of revision surgery is higher for Systemics and the more severe Intermediates. Most often, additional surgery is needed because polyps regrow, since surgery does not address the underlying cause of the polyp growth. The larger the polyps were to begin with, the more likely they are to regrow and eventually reobstruct the nose and sinuses. However, it's impossible to predict how quickly polyps will regrow to the point where revision surgery is needed—it could be as soon as a year or two or as long as twenty years.

The decision to get revision surgery is much like the decision to have surgery in the first place: it's a matter of quality of life. You should seriously consider it only if your symptoms are not responding to sinus medications and are significantly affecting your ability to function throughout the day.

The rate of success for revision surgery is lower than that for first-time sinus surgery. Still, the majority of patients do get significant improvement. The likelihood of success depends on the cause of failure. If it's an isolated scar band, the chances of improved sinus function once the band is cut are high. If, however, the sinus ostia are wide open on endoscopic examination and CT scan, but you are still having recurrent infections because of inflamed mucosa throughout the nose and sinuses, then the chances of additional surgery helping are lower. In that case, you should consider nonsurgical treatment options, including regular nasal saline irrigations, broad-spectrum antibiotic therapy (including topical or intravenous delivery methods, as discussed in Chapter 11), and evaluation for underlying allergic and immune disorders (as discussed in Chapters 4 and 19).

## What's Next

That completes our section on surgery. Next, we'll examine a phenomenon that has received a lot of attention from researchers and the media in recent years: fungal sinusitis.

# PART IV

# Special Considerations in Sinusitis

# CHAPTER 17

# Fungal Sinusitis

Bacteria aren't the only microorganisms that find the human body an inviting place to live. Fungi—forms of which exist in nature as mushrooms and in your bathtub as mildew—can be found in abundance on the body's surfaces, including the skin, mouth, and nasal passages. Bacteria and fungi share an important characteristic: most of the time they're unobtrusive visitors, but in the right circumstances, they can multiply, prompting discomfort and illness.

On the skin, an overgrowth of certain fungi causes everyday annoyances, such as athlete's foot and jock itch. Fungi's role in the nasal passages is a bit more complicated. We know that fungi can and do reside in both the nose and sinuses. But how often do fungi cause sinusitis?

That question has been the subject of great debate among researchers in recent years. A group of scientists at the Mayo Clinic challenged conventional wisdom that bacterial infections are the underlying cause of sinusitis and proposed that fungi were the true culprits in most cases. I'll cover this "fungal theory" in a bit, but first let's look at some scenarios where there's little doubt that fungi are directly related to the sinusitis.

## Types of Fungal Sinusitis

There are three types of infections in which unusually large numbers of fungi are present in the sinuses:

- fungus ball sinusitis
- allergic fungal sinusitis
- invasive fungal sinusitis

These three diagnoses account for less than 5 percent of all sinusitis cases.

### Fungus Ball Sinusitis

The fungi that normally live harmlessly inside your sinuses occasionally begin to multiply. Like a bacterial sinusitis, this process may be triggered by blockage of the sinus ostia. But instead of bacteria overgrowing, for some reason it's the fungi. Growth may be slow or rapid, but if it continues unchecked, the sinus eventually fills up with a ball of thick fungal debris. Much like a bacterial infection, this process can cause facial pain and pressure.

Fungus ball sinusitis is typically diagnosed by CT scan. Whereas a bacterial infection often shows fluid inside the sinus (due to the presence of pus), the fungus ball tends to be more solid in appearance. Also, unlike most forms of sinusitis, a fungus ball usually causes an infection in a single sinus, typically one of the maxillary sinuses.

Medications usually aren't effective against fungus ball sinusitis, so often the only option is a surgical procedure in which the fungus ball—a gelatinous, green mass—is scooped out of the sinus with a tool known as a curette. Following surgery, sinus function quickly returns to normal, and most patients need no further treatment. Individuals with fungus ball sinusitis fit into the category of Locals on the Sinusitis Spectrum.

### Allergic Fungal Sinusitis

Similar to pollen or dust allergies, people may have a reaction to the fungi living in their nose and sinuses, a condition known as allergic fungal sinusitis (AFS). The allergic reaction may cause the mucous membrane lining the sinuses to become inflamed. In addition, very thick mucus, called allergic mucin, collects within the sinus. This mucin is typically dark green in color, with the consistency of peanut butter. Many people with AFS also have polyps. The combination of mucin and polyps often blocks the sinus ostia, causing a secondary bacterial infection.

A CT scan usually reveals thick mucus and debris filling sinuses on both sides of the head. This debris is composed of white blood cells called eosinophils, as well as stringy filaments called hyphae, which are a form of the fungus. Because of the presence of eosinophils, AFS is also known as eosinophilic fungal rhinosinusitis.

Treatment usually starts with steroid sprays to shrink polyps and antibiotics to control any concurrent bacterial infection. In some cases, oral steroids successfully relieve symptoms. In most cases, however, surgery is eventually needed to clear the thick debris within the sinuses and remove any polyps. Although surgery has a high likelihood of improving symptoms for the short term, in many patients, the underlying allergic mechanism persists and infections return, requiring repeat procedures. On the Sinusitis Spectrum, those with AFS are considered Systemics.

## Invasive Fungal Sinusitis

The final type of fungal sinusitis is rare but potentially fatal. It occurs only in patients whose immune systems are severely compromised. Examples include individuals with HIV or AIDS; people who have uncontrolled diabetes; those receiving chemotherapy for cancer; and organ transplant recipients who are taking immunosuppressant drugs.

Because these patients' natural defense mechanisms are weakened, fungi are able to attack the sinus walls and invade the underlying blood vessels and bone. Uncontrolled infection can extend to the eyes, causing blindness, and to the brain, causing meningitis.

Invasive fungal sinusitis is diagnosed by a CT scan that shows destruction of the bony sinus walls and by examination that shows nonliving tissue in the nose of a severely ill patient. If a case is recognized early enough, radical surgery to remove the infected tissue in combination with intravenous antifungal agents can be lifesaving.

## A Larger Role for Fungi?

Some researchers believe fungi's role in sinusitis goes beyond the three types I've described. In fact, they think fungi cause almost all cases of chronic sinusitis.

This novel viewpoint made headlines in 1999, when researchers at the Mayo Clinic published a study showing fungi are present in mucus samples from nearly all patients with sinusitis. Until then, other researchers had mostly focused on tissue samples and pus (which contains bacteria) to diagnose sinusitis, but not mucus (which contains fungus).

The Minnesota researchers theorized that fungi trigger an influx of eosinophils in certain patients prone to sinus infections. These eosinophils attack the fungus by releasing inflammation-inducing substances, such as major basic protein (MBP), the presence of which irritates the sinus lining and puts patients at risk for a secondary bacterial infection. Treatment that focused on eliminating fungi, they said, would help huge numbers of patients whose sinusitis never seemed to go away.

A follow-up study from the Mayo Clinic suggested that people's symptoms improved when they irrigated their nose with topical antifungal agents. Because of this, many ENT doctors began treating their most difficult chronic sinusitis patients with nasal irrigations and nebulized solutions containing Amphotericin B (amphocin). Others placed these hard-to-treat patients on weeks or months of the oral antifungal medication itraconazole (Sporanox).

Despite the initial enthusiasm, subsequent results have been unimpressive. Many observers now attribute the early improvements seen in some patients to the cleansing effects of nasal irrigations rather than the antifungal agent. No controlled studies have emerged demonstrating the benefits of antifungal agents for the treatment of chronic sinusitis.

It is also noteworthy that the 1999 Mayo Clinic report showed the same fungi that were growing in sinusitis patients were also growing in the mucus of a control group of subjects who did not have sinusitis. Perhaps the fungi reside peacefully in all of our sinuses, just as they do in our mouths and on our skin, causing only occasional infections in select circumstances.

For now, the fungal theory of sinusitis remains controversial. I'm among the skeptics. I do believe eosinophils play an important role in the development of sinusitis, but I doubt that the presence of fungi is the "missing link" that explains why most people get sinusitis.

## What's Next

Next, we'll look at treatments for a deviated septum and other problems associated with sinusitis.

# CHAPTER 18

# The Deviated Septum and Other Sinus-Related Problems

Given the myriad of tiny structures and narrow passageways inside your nose and sinuses, it shouldn't be surprising that even a small change in the interior layout of your Nasal House can have significant effects on sinus function. Let's take a look at some of the anatomical problems that can trigger sinus infections.

## The Deviated Septum

As you'll recall from Chapter 2, the septum is a thin partition made of flexible cartilage in front and bone in back that divides the nose in half. While it's rare to have a perfectly straight septum, usually the bend is minor and inconsequential. However, if the bend is significant—what's known as a deviated septum—it can block breathing or the sinus ostia, leading to nasal congestion and infections (see Figure 18.1).

How do you get a deviated septum? There are two ways. Some people are born with one. As a baby travels down the birth canal, its head rotates, compressing the nose to one side. It's not uncommon for the soft cartilage in the front of the septum to get

**FIGURE 18.1** Deviated Septum

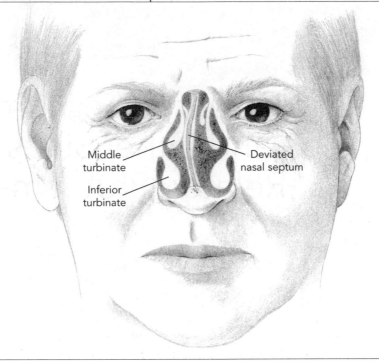

Middle
turbinate

Deviated
nasal septum

Inferior
turbinate

*A deviated nasal septum is a common cause of nasal obstruction and can contribute to sinusitis.*

pushed off the bony groove on which it rests and become deviated, blocking one nostril. If the deviation is severe, an ENT specialist may be called on to reposition it within the first days of life, but in most cases, doctors take a wait-and-see approach.

The other cause of a deviated septum is a blow to the nose. Often this trauma occurs during childhood, when the nasal bones are still relatively soft. All it takes is a face-first fall, a ball hitting the nose, or a collision with the head of a sibling while horsing around, to name only a few possibilities. A deviated septum can also occur in adulthood, as a result of nasal trauma during sports, auto accidents, and the like.

Regardless of when or how the trauma occurred, problems from a deviated septum often do not become apparent for many years. As a person ages, the ligaments that support the nose and septum become more lax, so the deviation tends to become more severe. Eventually, breathing becomes difficult to the point where it interferes with daily activity or sleeping, and the person seeks a doctor's advice.

In most cases, a deviated septum affects one side of the nose more than the other. Remember how the nasal cycle causes the side of the nose you breathe out of to switch back and forth about every six hours? Well, a person whose septum deviates to the right will have more difficulty breathing through the right nostril than the left most of the time.

Diagnosis of a deviated septum is relatively straightforward and can be made by an ENT specialist on a routine nasal exam. A sinus CT scan also shows the shape of the septum. But even if the septum is obviously crooked, steroid sprays and decongestants may be all that's needed to relieve congestion, especially if the deviation exists in conjunction with allergies or other causes of nasal swelling.

If medications don't work, then an ENT specialist can do a surgical procedure called a septoplasty, which is performed under either local or general anesthesia. The surgeon makes an incision just inside the nostril, temporarily lifts the mucous membranes on the septum, and shaves down or removes the portion of the cartilage and bone that's deviated. Sometimes the surgeon places dissolvable stitches or inserts nasal packing at the conclusion of the procedure.

After surgery, there's usually some swelling, which recedes over the next week or two. Complications are rare but may include bleeding and infection.

## Enlarged Turbinates

As you may recall, turbinates are thin plates of bone covered by mucous membranes that warm and humidify the air we breathe. There are three pairs of turbinates: the inferior, middle, and superior. The inferior turbinates are the largest.

Very large inferior turbinates are a common cause of blocked breathing. They usually get that way when years of nasal allergies result in permanent swelling of the turbinate mucous membranes, a condition called turbinate hypertrophy.

The inferior turbinates can be shrunk with an electric needle in a process called cauterization. There's also a relatively new option known as radiofrequency turbinate reduction, which delivers a measured dose of electrical energy to heat and shrink swollen turbinate tissue. Cauterization and radiofrequency turbinate reduction are usually done under local anesthesia.

Alternatively, enlarged inferior turbinates can be remedied with a surgical procedure known as turbinectomy, in which a portion of the obstructing turbinate bone and/or surrounding mucous membrane is removed. With the patient under general anesthesia, a surgeon trims the turbinates with a surgical scissors or a microdebrider.

The middle turbinates also can become large and block breathing. Unlike the inferior turbinates, however, their growth is usually the result of enlargement of the bone, not the membranes. The turbinate bone expands when an air-filled compartment develops inside of it. A widened middle turbinate, referred to as a concha bullosa, can compress the adjacent OMC, leading to recurrent bouts of sinusitis. Enlarged middle turbinates that are believed to be causing sinusitis are often trimmed or removed during sinus surgery.

Although turbinate reduction can provide tremendous benefit, it can actually make things worse if overdone, as you'll see in the next section.

## Empty Nose Syndrome

In the past, it was fairly routine for ENT doctors to remove the entire inferior turbinates during surgery, and they occasionally removed the middle and superior turbinates as well. We know now that removing too much turbinate bone and tissue from inside the nose can cause a troubling phenomenon called empty nose syndrome (ENS). To avoid this disorder, surgeons today are much more likely to leave the turbinates or at least a portion of them.

Nevertheless, some people who have had extensive nasal surgery struggle with ENS, which has several symptoms. Without turbinates, incoming air remains dry. Mucus tends to thicken and form crusts that are prime targets for bacterial overgrowth, leading to inflammation and infection. But the hallmark of ENS is a sense that you're not breathing well through your nose—even though you really are. Turbinates provide resistance to incoming air, so their absence prompts a disquieting feeling that you're not inhaling enough air. Paradoxically, people with ENS often say they feel congested, when in reality the problem is too much air flow.

Treatment involves keeping the nasal passages moist to ease the dryness-related symptoms. Saline irrigation should be done several times a day and can be supplemented with moisturizing nasal sprays. Infections usually can be kept to a minimum by applying an antibiotic ointment once or twice a day.

## Eustachian Tube Dysfunction

Because the ears, nose, and throat are all connected, it's not uncommon for problems in one area to spill over into another. One example is Eustachian tube dysfunction (ETD).

Eustachian tubes are narrow passageways that connect the inside of the ears to the back of the nose in an area known as the nasopharynx (refer back to Figure 2.2). These tubes equalize the pressure between your ears and the outside atmosphere. When you feel your ears popping in an elevator or on an airplane, that's your Eustachian tubes opening and closing.

ETD occurs when the Eustachian tubes become blocked and don't open properly. It can cause a buildup of pressure in the ears, leading to a sense of blockage, decreased hearing, and pain. This condition is likely to occur when you're flying while you have a cold and the plane begins to descend. However, anything that causes the inside of your nose to swell, including allergies and sinusitis, can also cause the Eustachian tubes to swell shut, leading to ETD.

With sinusitis, the increased mucus produced during an infection typically drains over the Eustachian tubes as it flows from the nose into the throat. This bacteria-laden drainage causes membranes that surround the Eustachian tubes to become inflamed, which prevents the tubes from opening. If fluid builds up in the ear, you can develop an ear infection on top of the sinus infection. The same antibiotics prescribed to treat sinus infections usually take care of ear infections as well.

In severe cases of ETD, a surgeon can insert tiny ventilation tubes made of plastic or metal through the eardrums to drain fluid and equalize pressure inside the ear. This procedure is commonly done in children with recurrent ear infections. A new surgery called Eustachian tuboplasty, in which the opening to the Eustachian tubes in the back of the nose is enlarged with a laser or microdebrider, is now being evaluated for the treatment of ETD.

## Triad Asthma

This disease gets its name from its three associated problems: asthma, aspirin sensitivity, and nasal polyps. Triad asthma, which is also referred to as Samter's triad or aspirin-induced asthma, is a relatively common disorder, thought to occur in up to 10 percent of those with asthma.

People with triad asthma have an overactive enzyme that leads to chronic inflammation of the mucous membranes in the sinuses and lungs. This enzyme, called 5-lipoxygenase, results in the overproduction of certain inflammation-causing substances called leukotrienes.

Although those with triad asthma do not have a true allergy to aspirin in the sense of an immune-triggered response, ingestion of even one aspirin can cause a serious asthma attack. Nonsteroidal anti-inflammatory drugs, such as ibuprofen (Advil,

Motrin) or naproxen (Aleve), can also trigger an attack, but it's usually less severe.

This disease typically arises in adults who were not previously known to be aspirin-sensitive, so anyone with nasal polyps who hasn't taken over-the-counter painkillers since childhood should do so with extreme caution.

The polyps associated with triad asthma usually grow so large that they obstruct nasal breathing and impair sense of smell. Although postnasal drainage is typically present, pain is usually minimal or absent. The standard regimen of sinusitis medications, including steroid sprays, are effective in some patients, but most require oral steroids, such as prednisone, to shrink their polyps significantly. Many of those with triad asthma elect to undergo surgery to remove the polyps and improve their quality of life. But no matter the treatment, the polyps usually regrow, requiring future courses of oral steroids and/or surgery.

## Vacuum Sinusitis

Vacuum sinusitis is a peculiar ailment in which a person seems to develop sinusitis symptoms without having an infection. We're not even 100 percent sure it exists, but we do know people sometimes have:

- symptoms of sinusitis, particularly facial pain, which temporarily get better when they take sinus medications
- a normal CT scan that shows no obstructions of sinus ostia

One possible explanation is that these patients actually have intermittent blockage—one day the doors are shut, the next they're open, and the next after that they're shut again. So a CT scan taken on a day when the ostia happen to be open will not show an obstruction.

In these patients, when the ostia shut, it's thought that the interior lining of the sinuses absorbs the oxygen in the sinuses. The resulting negative pressure forms a vacuum in the sinuses that causes pain.

Because vacuum sinusitis is not well understood, ENT doctors are generally reluctant to operate on patients who have normal CT scans. Instead, we usually try steroids and decongestants. In addition, we look for another diagnosis that may be causing sinusitis-like symptoms, such as migraines, neuritis, or neuralgia, as discussed in Chapter 20.

## Sinus Tumors

People commonly worry about tumors when they get sick—it's human nature. When it comes to sinus tumors, there are three important facts to keep in mind. First, they're extremely rare. Second, when they do occur, they're nearly always benign. Third, both benign and malignant (meaning cancerous) sinus tumors usually are detected early because they block the nose and sinuses, causing the same symptoms as an infection.

A benign tumor is an abnormal mass that enlarges but does not spread (or metastasize) to other areas of the body. Note that *benign* is not synonymous with *harmless*. Just by getting bigger, a benign sinus tumor can do a lot of damage. In rare cases, if left untreated, it can even be fatal.

The most common benign tumor of the sinuses is known as an inverted papilloma. This type of tumor can usually be completely removed with surgery through the nostril using an endoscope. To ensure that 100 percent of the tumor is removed, the surgeon cuts out both the tumor and some healthy surrounding tissue; if even one cell is left behind, the tumor will grow back. We don't know what causes benign tumors to develop.

A malignant tumor is a growth that will metastasize to distant sites in the body. Cancerous tumors are often evident on a CT scan because of their destructive appearance, such as erosion through the bony sinus walls.

There are several types of malignant sinus tumors, including squamous cell carcinoma (the type associated with most lung cancers) and adenocarcinoma (the type found in most breast cancers). Studies have shown that smokers and people whose work exposes them to wood dust, leather, glue, nickel, or chromium have an elevated risk for malignant sinus tumors.

These malignancies are usually treated with a combination of surgery and radiation. When detected early, many cancerous sinus tumors can be successfully treated and do not return.

## What's Next

Next, we'll take a look at some special circumstances of sinusitis, such as sinus infections in children and pregnant women.

# CHAPTER 19

# Special Circumstances of Sinusitis

Now that we've examined treatments for the most common forms of sinusitis, it's a good time to look at some special circumstances.

## Children and Sinusitis

Like adults, children can develop sinus infections. Most often, kids' infections follow on the heels of a cold, but they can also be triggered by allergies. Although the infection process is the same as in grown-ups, several factors specific to children affect the way we diagnose and treat pediatric sinusitis.

First, doctors have a harder time distinguishing between a child's sinusitis and severe cold or allergies. In an infant or a young child, the only symptom of sinusitis that parents may notice is green nasal drainage, a nighttime cough, fever, or increased irritability. Physicians, meanwhile, usually do not have the benefit of a sinus CT scan. This tool is only used for the most persistent cases because we are hesitant to expose the child's developing body to radiation.

So, faced with the never-ending supply of runny-nosed children, pediatricians must use clinical judgment to make their best assessment and treat the illness. Over-the-counter medications combining decongestants, antihistamines, and cough suppressants are helpful for both colds and sinusitis. Antibiotics are prescribed when symptoms persist and sinusitis seems probable.

Another difference is that sinus surgery is performed much less commonly in children than in adults. It's only done in the most severe cases in which antibiotics don't work and a CT scan shows definite sinus obstruction. And even in these cases, patience may pay off. Children catch fewer colds as they age and frequently outgrow their allergies, so the number of sinus infections often will drop without surgical intervention.

But when sinus surgery is performed on children, it can be just as successful as in adults. Children heal faster from surgery and are usually back to school within three to five days. Young children are often unwilling to undergo postoperative cleaning in the office under local anesthesia; such cases may require a second trip to the operating room one week after surgery for cleaning under general anesthesia.

While sinus surgery on children is rare, another type of surgery related to the sinuses is not (see the sidebar "Adenoidectomy").

Because cystic fibrosis arises in childhood and commonly causes nasal polyps, children with polyps need a test that analyzes the amount of salt in their perspiration to determine if they have

## Adenoidectomy

The adenoids are a lump of tissue at the back of the nose that contains cells designed to fight infection. They actually consist of the same tissue as tonsils. In some children, the adenoids grow so large that they block the nose and sinuses, causing snoring, persistent nasal discharge, and sinusitis. Swollen adenoids can also harbor bacteria, causing repeated sinus and ear infections. If the adenoid tissue remains large after repeated doses of antibiotics, surgery to remove it can usually eliminate the problem. It's a relatively brief procedure that's done on an outpatient basis.

this disorder (see the section "Genetic Causes of Sinusitis" a little later in this chapter).

## Sinusitis During Pregnancy

Women's bodies tend to retain fluid during pregnancy, and among the tissues that become swollen are the mucous membranes lining the nose and sinuses. Similar to a cold or allergies, this swelling can block the sinus ostia and trigger an infection. As a result, it's not uncommon for women with sinusitis to have more flare-ups than usual during pregnancy.

Treatment of pregnant women is complicated by physicians' reluctance to prescribe medication, since we don't want to risk harming the developing fetus. As a general rule, pregnant women should not take medication during the first trimester and should use caution thereafter. However, an untreated infection that persists also presents risks to the fetus, especially if it causes a fever, so exceptions are sometimes necessary.

If you are pregnant and have a persistent sinus infection, check with your obstetrician before taking any medication. Obstetricians often will OK use of medications that have been used for decades and have a safe pregnancy profile, such as the decongestant pseudoephedrine and the antibiotic amoxicillin.

On the plus side, once a pregnant woman with sinusitis symptoms gives birth, the fluid retention recedes and the sinusitis usually subsides.

## Genetic Causes of Sinusitis

Although it's likely that many genetic links to sinusitis will be found in the future, for now these are the two we know the most about.

### Cystic Fibrosis (CF)

This inherited disorder, which is usually diagnosed in childhood, is caused by a genetic defect (called a DNA mutation) that leads to abnormal secretions in various organs of the body, including the lungs, pancreas, liver, and reproductive tract. In the respiratory system, this dysfunction produces very thick mucus, which can block the lungs and sinuses, triggering pneumonia and sinusitis. More than 90 percent of patients with CF have chronic sinusitis; large nasal polyps are also common. Many need sinus surgery to clear the polyps, which often regrow, requiring repeated surgery.

Although in the past most people with CF did not survive into adulthood, treatments have become so effective in recent years that many CF patients are now living well into middle age. In addition, some children and adults are now being diagnosed with a milder form of CF that is caused by a partial defect in the DNA gene; it's less likely to affect longevity, but secretions can still be thick, causing frequent bouts of sinusitis.

### Primary Ciliary Dyskinesia (PCD)

As you may recall from Chapter 2, the lungs, nose, and sinuses are lined with microscopic hairs called cilia, which beat rhythmically, clearing mucus and debris from air passages. PCD, also known as immotile-cilia syndrome or Kartagener's syndrome, is a genetic disorder that results in a structural defect in the cilia, leaving them unable to beat properly. Mucus builds up within the sinuses, leading to chronic infections and the formation of nasal polyps.

As with CF, this genetic defect can cause problems throughout the body. Its effect on the lungs means people with PCD are prone to chronic cough and recurrent bouts of pneumonia. Medications can provide some improvement. Sinus surgery to remove the polyps and clear the sinuses is effective but usually needs to be repeated.

## Sarcoidosis

Sarcoidosis is a rare illness that produces small beadlike patches of inflamed tissue known as granulomas throughout the body. These granulomas are most common in the lungs but can also occur in the nasal passages, triggering sinus inflammation and infection.

The cause of sarcoidosis is not known, but it's believed to be due to an abnormal stimulation of the immune system. It occurs three to four times more frequently in blacks and is also more common in women than in men.

In some cases, people find out they have sarcoidosis after surgery for sinusitis, when microscopic examination of the removed tissue reveals granulomas. More commonly, it's picked up during a routine chest x-ray.

Sarcoidosis produces a cobblestone appearance of the nasal mucosa, which is visible during endoscopic examination. If an ENT doctor suspects sarcoidosis as a cause of sinusitis, the diagnosis can be confirmed by a biopsy of the nasal tissue. The diagnosis can also be confirmed by a blood test known as an ACE level, which measures the amount of angiotensin converting enzyme in the blood, a substance known to be elevated in those with this disease.

Sarcoidosis can often be treated with oral steroids to reduce inflammation throughout the body. In more severe cases affecting the sinuses, surgery may be needed to relieve obstruction caused by inflammation and scarring.

## Wegener's Granulomatosis

Wegener's is another rare disease that causes granulomas to form throughout the body, including the nose and sinuses. Here, however, the granulomas damage the walls of small- and medium-sized blood vessels. This damage interferes with normal blood supply, which can lead to injury and destruction of nearby tissues. The cause of Wegener's is also unknown, but research suggests it's an immune disorder in which the body's defenses are mistakenly aimed at the blood vessels.

Wegener's most commonly affects three areas: the lungs, the kidneys, and the nose and sinuses. Unlike most people with sinusitis, whose nasal membranes are swollen and secrete too much mucus, those with Wegener's have excessively thin and dry nasal tissues. The blood vessels in these membranes become fragile, leading to frequent nosebleeds. What mucus there is in the nose tends to dry out, leading to the formation of crusts. More advanced cases of Wegener's cause erosion of cartilage in the nose, resulting in a hole in the septum (also known as a septal perforation).

Sinus infections are common among people with Wegener's, and the disease is often diagnosed during treatment for sinusitis. An ENT doctor who suspects a patient has Wegener's will order a series of blood tests, including one that detects the presence of antineutrophil cytoplasmic antibody, a marker for Wegener's. The diagnosis can also be confirmed with a biopsy of tissue from a turbinate.

Wegener's is treated with oral steroids and medications known as immunosuppressive agents, which blunt the response of the body's immune system. With treatment, more than 90 percent of people with Wegener's enter remission, although as many as half will relapse when medication is reduced or stopped. Those who do not relapse may remain in remission for many years, often without needing more medication. Like sarcoidosis, sinus surgery is reserved for those cases in which the sinuses become blocked by diseased tissue.

## Immune Deficiency Syndromes

Your body depends on an intact immune system to fight infections. This system functions by the complex interaction of many components, including white blood cells known as T lymphocytes and B lymphocytes. It is the B lymphocytes that produce antibodies, specialized molecules essential for the identification and destruction of foreign substances such as bacteria.

With certain inherited diseases, one or more of these components are missing and the body cannot mount an effective immune response. In rare cases, such as with the disease known as severe combined immunodeficiency, even a simple infection can be fatal. You may remember the 1970s movie *The Boy in the Plastic Bubble*, about a child with this disorder.

Less severe but more common immune deficiencies also exist, and they may affect the sinuses. One example is a disorder known as IgG subclass deficiency. IgG is the name of the most common type of antibody. People with low levels of this antibody often have a history of recurrent bouts of pneumonia and sinusitis.

A diagnosis of immune deficiency may be considered in cases in which a CT scan fails to show any obstructions that would trigger sinus infections. In other words, the sinus doors are open and the ostiomeatal complex is clear, but the person's sinuses nonetheless are perpetually infected. Such infections are believed to occur in these people because their immune systems are incapable of keeping the bacteria that normally exist in the sinuses in check.

Immune deficiencies are diagnosed by tests that measure the amount of white blood cells and antibodies in the blood. If these tests reveal low levels of IgG, treatment to replace the antibody through monthly transfusions of IgG may be initiated.

## What's Next

Next, we'll look at some disorders that seem like sinusitis—but aren't.

# CHAPTER 20

# Disorders That Mimic Sinusitis

When a person has three common sinusitis symptoms—congestion, postnasal drip, and headache—it seems logical to conclude that he or she has sinusitis. But sometimes what seems logical is still wrong.

How can this be? In some cases, a person has more than one health ailment, so a constellation of symptoms that are actually unrelated seem connected, and what seems like sinusitis isn't really sinusitis at all. Let's take a look at some of the most common examples where patients and doctors may mistake other diseases for sinusitis.

## Reflux

Reflux occurs when acid and other digestive juices in the stomach flow upward instead of downward. No doubt you've heard of the most common type, gastroesophageal reflux disease (GERD), which causes heartburn and can damage the tube connecting the throat and stomach (the esophagus) if left untreated.

There's also a lesser known kind of reflux called laryngopharyngeal reflux (LPR), in which stomach acid continues through the esophagus and travels up to the voice box (larynx) and the back of your throat (pharynx). LPR does not usually cause heartburn. As a result, it's sometimes referred to as silent reflux. Instead, it tends to cause symptoms like hoarseness, constant throat clearing, and the feeling of a foreign body in the throat just below the Adam's apple.

Because reflux brings secretions to the back of the throat, it can feel like postnasal drip, one of sinusitis's key symptoms. But the drainage doesn't get better with typical sinus medications, such as nasal steroid sprays, antihistamines, and mucus-thinning agents.

An ENT specialist can diagnose reflux if an exam shows inflammation of the back wall of the larynx and pharynx. To confirm the diagnosis, your doctor may want to look directly into the esophagus with a flexible endoscope or measure the acidity (pH) of liquids in the esophagus with a probe.

Treatment for GERD and LPR starts with lifestyle and dietary changes. These simple antireflux precautions can lead to dramatic improvement:

- Avoid foods that cause reflux, such as alcohol and caffeine.
- Do not eat before bedtime so less acid is secreted while you sleep.
- Elevate the head of the bed so your head is above your stomach during the night. (You can best do this by putting wooden blocks under the legs at the head of the bed or by sleeping with your upper body on a solid foam wedge.)

Taking an antacid like Mylanta or Maalox one hour after meals and before bedtime can complement these measures. If symptoms persist, acid-reducing medications are available over the counter or by prescription. There are two basic types: H2-blockers (including Pepcid, Tagamet, and Zantac) and proton pump inhibitors (such as Nexium, Prilosec, and Protonix).

One final gastrointestinal note. Some physicians believe there is, in fact, a strong connection between reflux and sinusitis. They have proposed that most cases of sinusitis are caused by acid and other gastric contents flowing all the way up to the nose and sinuses at night, but this theory remains untested.

## Dental Disease and TMJ

Certain dental disorders can mimic sinusitis. A common example is an infection of the root of a tooth in the upper jaw. Because the roots of these teeth are adjacent to the floor of the maxillary sinus, such infections can cause pain that radiates to the cheek and closely resembles sinusitis.

Inflammation of the jaw joint, called the temporomandibular joint, or TMJ, can also cause facial pain that mimics sinusitis. You can feel the TMJ move by putting a finger just in front of your ear and opening and closing your mouth. Soreness or clicking in this region may indicate an abnormality.

TMJ pain can result from a variety of causes, including unconsciously grinding your teeth while sleeping and arthritis of the jaw joint. Whatever the cause, initial treatment involves a soft diet (no apples or steaks), warm compresses over the joint, and an anti-inflammatory medication (like Advil or Motrin). If that doesn't work, a dentist can fashion a plastic mouth guard that resembles a retainer commonly used by teenagers who have had braces. This device, which is worn at night to take pressure off the TMJ, is highly successful at relieving the associated discomfort. In the most extreme cases, an oral surgeon can operate on the TMJ to smooth irregularities of cartilage and bone within the joint.

Interestingly, the confusion between dental and sinus problems goes both ways. It's not uncommon for a maxillary sinus infection to be mistaken for a dental problem, because pain in this sinus can radiate to the upper teeth. When this happens, a dentist may pull a healthy tooth and even perform an unnecessary root canal. A dental x-ray or sinus CT scan can usually determine which is the true source of the pain.

## Migraines

Migraines are a common cause of headaches, occurring in about 10 percent of the population. They usually cause a severe, throbbing pain, most often on one side of the head. A migraine headache can last hours or even days and can be associated with nausea and light sensitivity. Some people know when a migraine is about to start because they experience vision changes (known as an aura), commonly dark patterns or wavy lines in the corner of their eyes.

Migraines used to be referred to as vascular headaches because they were thought to result from abnormal dilation of blood vessels. However, recent research has not supported this theory, and their actual cause remains unknown.

A migraine can be confused with sinusitis because nasal discharge often accompanies the headache. However, unlike sinusitis, the drainage from a migraine is usually clear and one-sided. Also, the pain from migraines is more likely to be located on the side of the head, whereas sinus headaches tend to occur in the forehead region or the back of the head. In addition, migraines are likely to affect only one side of the head, whereas sinus headaches usually occur on both sides.

A variant known as facial migraine can be mistaken for maxillary sinusitis because it causes pain in the cheeks and/or forehead. This entity is a real possibility when patients have facial pain but their sinus CT scans are clear.

Migraines can sometimes be prevented by identifying and avoiding what triggers an episode, such as caffeine, alcohol, certain foods, and stress. If this approach does not work, over-the-counter migraine medications may help, as well as prescription drugs available through your primary care physician or neurologist.

Although sinusitis and migraines are two separate entities, for some people the two ailments appear to be related. It's not uncommon for sinus infections to trigger migraine headaches. In these cases, getting better control of sinusitis often leads to a reduction in the frequency of migraines.

## Neuritis

Neuritis refers to inflammation of nerve endings that can trigger pain anywhere in the body. When the pain involves nerves in the face or head, it can be mistaken for a symptom of sinusitis. There are many causes of neuritis, including viral infection, diabetes, immune disorders, and trauma. Neuritis affecting nerves in the nose can sometimes occur after sinus surgery.

A common treatment for neuritis is antiseizure medications (such as Neurontin) that were developed to treat people with epilepsy. Because the pain from neuritis is chronic, medications containing narcotics are best avoided, to prevent the possibility of addiction. Injections into the specific area of facial pain with anesthetics, steroids, and Botox (see the sidebar "Botox for Facial Pain") have also proved successful.

## Botox for Facial Pain

Botox injections have gained widespread popularity in recent years as a treatment for facial wrinkles. This medication is derived from botulinum toxin, a deadly poison that may contaminate improperly canned foods. When injected in minute amounts just below the skin, Botox paralyzes the underlying facial muscles that cause wrinkles to form. Because this paralysis eventually wears off, Botox must be injected every four to six months to maintain the cosmetic effect.

We don't know exactly how Botox works to ward off facial pain, but it's thought to block the transmission of nerve impulses affecting pain receptors. When it works, injections often need to be repeated. In any case, if you suffer from facial pain that doesn't respond to medication, Botox could conceivably help you feel better—and look younger at the same time.

## Neuralgia

*Neuralgia* literally means "nerve pain." Like neuritis, it has many different causes and can be confused with sinusitis when it affects the face or head. Trigeminal neuralgia—a condition affecting the trigeminal nerve, which supplies sensation to much of the face— is the most common type of neuralgia in this region. It usually involves intermittent episodes of brief, sharp, intense pain affecting one side of the face.

One popular theory attributes trigeminal neuralgia to an abnormally shaped blood vessel pressing against the nerve. Like neuritis, it can be treated with medications and injections, but surgery to identify and move the abnormal blood vessel from the trigeminal nerve has also been successful in many people with this disorder.

## Atypical Facial Pain

When physicians are unable to determine the specific source of a person's facial pain, they may make a diagnosis of atypical facial pain. In other words, we just don't understand the cause.

For patients with persistent facial pain that has not responded to standard therapy, a multidisciplinary pain clinic is often the best option. These clinics, which draw on the combined expertise of specialists (such as anesthesiologists, neurologists, ENT doctors, physical therapists, and psychologists) are becoming more commonplace in large hospitals and referral centers. They offer the latest in diagnostic and treatment techniques for patients suffering from bodily pain.

## What's Next

What does the future hold for sinusitis treatment? In our final chapter, we'll look at what's on the horizon.

# CHAPTER 21

# Future Considerations: Where Do We Go from Here?

If in 1975 a person with sinusitis somehow magically fast-forwarded herself to the office of a present-day ENT doctor, she would be in for some pleasant surprises. Between CT scans, nasal endoscopes, and advances in surgery, the diagnostic and treatment options for sinusitis have improved dramatically.

Now, what if today's patient were thrust thirty years into the future? I suspect there will be even greater progress. In the next few decades, I see important developments affecting sinus treatment in three areas: gene therapy, computerized surgery, and new classes of sinus medications.

## Genomics and Gene Therapy

No doubt you've heard about the mapping of the human genome and gene therapy, both of which are aspects of an emerging field known as genomics. Basically, every cell in your body contains strands of DNA, genetic material that carries the code for about thirty thousand genes. These genes create a detailed and specific pattern of proteins that serve as the body's building blocks to make you the unique individual that you are. They are responsible for your eye and hair color, as well as sinus-related issues like allergies and a tendency to grow polyps. Abnormalities in this pattern, such as a missing or extra gene, are associated with inherited diseases.

Sinus infections result from numerous diseases, some of which are genetic in origin. We've discussed a few, including cystic fibrosis and primary ciliary dyskinesia, but it's likely there are dozens of other, more subtle ones that have yet to be identified.

At the moment, we only see the result: inflamed mucous membranes, thick mucus, and nasal polyps. But with the help of genomics, we should be able to gain insight into the specific gene or group of genes responsible for this symptom complex known as sinusitis.

So instead of our current shorthand of three categories of sinusitis patients—Locals, Intermediates, and Systemics—we might have twenty or thirty different types, identified with a number and letter system. A patient with a certain genetic pattern of sinusitis genes might be classified as having Type 1A Sinusitis, while another has Type 2C.

Diagnosis will be done on the basis of a blood or tissue sample, which is placed on a tiny chip, called a DNA microarray, and analyzed by a computer. In theory, you would immediately learn which type of sinusitis you have. Armed with this information, your physician would know which medications are most likely to be effective for your condition, and whether you'll benefit from surgery.

If the computer analysis reveals that your inflammation was triggered by a missing or defective gene, a normal copy of the gene could be incorporated into your cells by means of an injection or a tissue transplant, potentially curing you entirely of sinusitis. To date, much of the research into gene therapy has focused on life-threatening diseases, such as cancer. Now, researchers are starting to focus more attention on chronic diseases, including diabetes and sinusitis.

## Computerized and Robotic Surgery

Here, I'm not talking about a Jetsons-style world in which human-sized robots mingle with people at the supermarket and perform surgery in the operating room. It's just a matter of computers and high technology playing an even greater role in surgery than they already do.

We now have image-guided surgery that allows the surgeon to navigate through a three-dimensional view of the patient's sinuses from a computerized CT scan. Although this device can be tremendously helpful, it has limitations. For example, the CT image is a static snapshot of the patient's past, which fails to reflect changes that occur as the surgeon operates, removing bone and tissue.

The next step will be a real-time CT or MRI scan that's instantly updated during surgery. This technology is already being used for certain types of neurosurgery and should be available to sinus surgeons in the not too distant future. Such a device will help the surgeon remove all diseased tissue and reduce the risk of complications.

Somewhat farther down the line, we can expect to see greater use of computer-directed surgical tools (robotics). Humans have certain physical limitations that robots do not. For instance, our wrists can only rotate so far, and we have slight tremors. By contrast, a robotic arm can rotate 360 degrees without a tremor, allowing for more delicate and precise manipulations than humanly possible.

So in the operating room of the future, the surgeon will be sitting in front of a computer screen showing a three-dimensional view of the patient's nasal passages. The surgeon will manipulate a control panel with highly calibrated joystick controls not unlike what you see on today's video games. This robotic technology has already been introduced for some abdominal, orthopedic, and heart surgical procedures. It's only a matter of time before it's applied to sinus surgery, where precise and delicate manipulations are critical.

## New Medications

While computers will help make surgery safer and more efficient, I expect that operations for sinusitis will actually become much less common in the future. Surgery will still be needed for those whose sinusitis stems from anatomical abnormalities present at birth or caused by trauma later in life. But most of the people we currently consider Intermediates and Systemics won't need surgery, because of the introduction of new medications and techniques that address the root cause of an individual's sinusitis.

The continued development of longer-acting and more broad-spectrum antibiotics is one example where drug development will be helpful in the near future. But the biggest impact on sinusitis over the next ten years is likely to be the development of whole new classes of medications that reduce inflammation and shrink or prevent polyps. Trials are currently under way to test the effectiveness of drugs that block the inflammatory response (including one called anti-IL5) and inhibit the immune trigger (including one called anti-IgE) that can lead to sinusitis. Another trial is planned to study the effectiveness of a drug called imatinib in patients with sinusitis. This medication is known to block the formation of eosinophils, key inflammatory cells found in diseased sinus tissue. Ultimately, the continued development of improved drug delivery systems—such as time-release oral medications and patches worn on the skin that release a continual low dose—will free people from having to take these and other new medications every day.

## Farewell Remarks

I hope you benefited from reading this book and will now be spurred to pursue the care best suited for your sinusitis. Whether it's sinus irrigation, a new medication, a change in diet, or surgery, the important thing is to never give up. I can't tell you how many times patients who have struggled with sinusitis for years ultimately find relief through the treatments discussed in this book.

I wish you the best of luck at healing your sinuses.

# Glossary

**acute sinusitis:** sinusitis that lasts three months or less

**adenoid:** lump of tissue at the back of the nose that contains cells designed to fight infection; enlarged adenoids can block nasal breathing, particularly in children

**adenoidectomy:** surgery to remove the adenoids

**allergen:** substance that triggers an allergy

**allergic fungal sinusitis:** type of sinusitis caused by a reaction to fungus in the sinuses

**allergic rhinitis:** inflammation of the nasal passages caused by an allergic reaction; may be seasonal or perennial (year-round)

**allergy:** sensitivity to certain substances in the environment, such as pollens, foods, or microorganisms, that trigger a response by the immune system; may cause nasal congestion, sneezing, and itching; may trigger sinusitis

**amoxicillin:** antibiotic frequently prescribed for sinus infections; a variant of penicillin

**anaphylaxis:** serious allergic reaction involving the onset of hives, swelling of the throat, and difficulty breathing; occurs rarely as a side effect to certain medications and foods; caused by aspirin in people with triad asthma

**anosmia:** loss of the sense of smell

**antibody:** molecule that plays a key role in the immune system's response to foreign substances, including allergens and bacteria

**aspirin-induced asthma:** see *triad asthma*

**atypical facial pain:** diagnosis given when facial pain has an unknown cause; may be mistaken for sinusitis

**bromelain:** compound present in pineapples that may reduce sinusitis symptoms

**capsaicin:** natural substance found in spicy foods, such as hot chili peppers; may temporarily relieve nasal congestion

**cephalosporin:** class of antibiotic often used to treat sinusitis; an alternative to penicillin variants

**chronic sinusitis:** sinusitis that lasts more than three months

**cilia:** tiny hairs that sweep mucus; cilia that line the interior of the sinuses propel mucus and entrapped debris out of the sinuses and into the nasal cavity

**computed tomography:** see *CT scan*

**computer-assisted surgery (CAS):** see *image-guided surgery*

**concha bullosa:** enlarged middle turbinate caused by the development of an air-filled compartment inside; may obstruct the sinuses

**congeners:** natural by-products of the fermentation process that are found in alcoholic beverages; may trigger sinusitis symptoms

**CT scan:** x-ray technique (using computed tomography) in which a series of cross-sectional images can be used to construct a three-dimensional view of a body structure; also known as CAT scan

**cyst:** closed sac containing fluid; commonly seen in the maxillary sinuses as the result of a blocked mucus-secreting gland

**cystic fibrosis:** hereditary disease characterized by the production of abnormally thick mucus, resulting in chronic respiratory infections and sinusitis

**deviated septum:** nasal septum that is not straight; may cause blocked breathing and sinusitis

**Draf 3 procedure:** see *frontal sinus drillout*

**empty nose syndrome (ENS):** condition that results from removal of too much bone and tissue during nasal surgery; may cause excessive nasal dryness

**endoscope:** see *nasal endoscope*

**endoscopic sinus surgery (ESS):** operation in which a surgeon passes an endoscope and small instruments through the nostrils to visualize and open areas of sinus blockage

**ENT doctor:** physician specializing in diseases of the ears, nose, and throat; also known as an otolaryngologist

**eosinophil:** type of white blood cell that plays a key role in allergic reactions and sinus inflammation

**epistaxis:** nosebleed

**ESS:** see *endoscopic sinus surgery*

**ethmoid sinuses:** pair of sinuses between the eyes, comprising five to ten little chambers on each side

**Eustachian tube dysfunction (ETD):** obstruction of the Eustachian tubes causing a sense of ear blockage or pressure; may lead to impaired hearing; may occur during a sinus infection

**Eustachian tubes:** passageways connecting the ears to the back of the nose; serve to equalize pressure in the ears

**FESS:** functional endoscopic sinus surgery; same as *endoscopic sinus surgery (ESS)*

**fibrosis:** formation of scar tissue; fibrosis following sinus surgery may lead to reobstruction of the sinuses, requiring revision surgery

**frontal sinus drillout:** surgical procedure in which the bony floor of the frontal sinus is removed to maximize mucus drainage; also known as Draf 3 or Modified Lothrop procedure

**frontal sinuses:** sinuses located within the frontal bone of the forehead

**fungal ball sinusitis:** type of sinusitis caused by fungus that grows into a ball-shaped mass, usually within the maxillary sinuses

**gastroesophageal reflux disease (GERD):** backward flow of stomach contents into the esophagus resulting from improper functioning of a sphincter at the lower end of the esophagus; may cause symptoms similar to sinusitis

**gene:** segment of DNA that codes for a particular protein; proteins serve as the building blocks of the body and form enzymes that trigger essential chemical reactions at the cellular level

**gene therapy:** insertion of genetic material into cells to replace malfunctioning genes for the treatment of genetic disorders

**genomics:** branch of medicine dealing with mapping all the genes in the body to diagnose and treat genetic causes of disease, including sinusitis

**GERD:** see *gastroesophageal reflux disease*

**granuloma:** small, beadlike patch of inflamed cells

**guaifenesin:** active ingredient in medication used to thin mucus

**homeopathy:** treatment of disease by administration of minute doses of a remedy that would in healthy persons produce symptoms similar to those of the disease; an alternative form of therapy to conventional medicine

**hypertrophy:** enlargement or swelling of tissue; in the nose and sinuses, hypertrophy of turbinates and mucous membranes may cause obstruction, triggering sinusitis

**image-guided surgery:** technique in which a computer tracking system and three-dimensional video display enable a surgeon to monitor the precise location of instruments within the nose during sinus surgery; also known as computer-assisted surgery or navigational surgery

**immotile-cilia syndrome:** see *primary ciliary dyskinesia*

**Intermediates:** individuals on the Sinusitis Spectrum whose symptoms fall between those of Locals and Systemics

**invasive fungal sinusitis:** rare type of sinusitis in which fungus invades through the sinus walls, destroying underlying bone and blood vessels; occurs in people whose immune systems are impaired

**irrigation:** see *nasal irrigation*

**Kartagener's syndrome:** see *primary ciliary dyskinesia*

**lamina papyracea:** thin bone that separates the ethmoid sinus and the eye socket

**laryngopharyngeal reflux (LPR):** backward flow of stomach contents up to the voice box (larynx) and the back of the throat (pharynx); can produce symptoms similar to sinusitis; also known as silent reflux

**leukotrienes:** substances released by white blood cells to fight infection as part of the immune response; cause inflammation of the nasal and sinus tissue

**Locals:** individuals on the Sinusitis Spectrum whose disease is caused by site-specific physical abnormalities within their nose or sinuses, such as a deviated septum or inflamed tissue limited to the region of the OMC

**LPR:** see *laryngopharyngeal reflux*

**lymphocyte:** type of white blood cell that plays a key role in the immune system and its response to infections

**macrolide:** class of antibiotic commonly used for patients with sinusitis who are allergic to penicillin

**magnetic resonance imaging (MRI):** radiological technique that uses a powerful magnet and radio waves to visualize body structures; not used for patients with routine sinus disease because of its inability to visualize bony structures, including the sinus walls

**maxillary sinuses:** sinuses located behind the cheekbones, extending from beneath the eyes to above the upper teeth

**meatus:** opening or passage in the body; the nasal cavity has three meatuses—the inferior, middle, and superior—each located beside its corresponding turbinate

**microdebrider:** thin hollow tube with a rotating blade at one end and a suction device at the other; used during sinus surgery to remove diseased tissue; also known as a microdissector or shaver

**microdissector:** see *microdebrider*

**migraine:** condition marked by recurrent, severe headaches; may be mistaken for sinus pain

**Modified Lothrop procedure:** see *frontal sinus drillout*

**MRI:** see *magnetic resonance imaging*

**mucociliary clearance:** process in which a blanket of mucus containing bacteria and debris is continuously swept out of a sinus by cilia lining the sinus interior; necessary part of healthy sinus function

**mucosa:** see *mucous membrane*

**mucous membrane:** thin sheet of tissue rich in glands that secrete mucus; mucous membranes line the nose and sinuses, as well as much of the respiratory and digestive tracts; also known as *mucosa*

**mucus:** substance produced by mucous membranes inside the nose and sinuses that helps provide moisture and entrap foreign particles

**nasal cycle:** normal phenomenon in which the dominant side for breathing through the nose switches from one side to the other; typically occurs about every six hours

**nasal endoscope:** thin high-resolution telescope used by a physician to examine the interior of the nose; also used for visualization during endoscopic sinus surgery

**nasal irrigation:** practice of washing out excess mucus from the nasal cavity with salt water; also known as nasal lavage or nasal rinsing

**nasal lavage:** see *nasal irrigation*

**nasal rinsing:** see *nasal irrigation*

**nasal septum:** approximately three-inch-long partition consisting of bone and cartilage that separates the nose into two roughly equal-sized nasal cavities

**nasal steroids:** potent anti-inflammatory agents that reduce swelling; available in topical form as nasal sprays

**nasal tape:** over-the-counter product designed to widen the nasal valve and improve breathing; also known as nasal strips

**nasal valve:** narrow region of the nasal cavity located in the middle third of the nose; a common area for nasal obstruction to occur

**neti pot:** small cup with a handle on one end and a spout on the other; used for nasal irrigation

**neuralgia:** nerve pain; neuralgia affecting the face may be mistaken for sinusitis

**neuritis:** inflammation of the nerve endings; neuritis affecting the face may be mistaken for sinusitis

**OMC:** see *ostiomeatal complex*

**ostia:** openings in a body part; the sinus ostia function as doors through which mucus drains from the sinuses into the nose

**ostiomeatal complex (OMC):** series of narrow channels and openings that serve as a common drainage pathway for the ethmoid, maxillary, and frontal sinuses; obstruction of the ostiomeatal complex is a common cause of sinusitis

**ostium:** singular form of *ostia*

**otolaryngologist:** physician specializing in diseases of the ears, nose, and throat; synonymous with *ENT doctor*

**pansinusitis:** sinusitis in which all four pairs of sinuses are infected

**phlegm:** mucus that collects in the throat; may accumulate during a bout of sinusitis

**polyp:** grapelike growth attached by a stalk to the mucous membrane lining the sinuses; commonly seen in patients with chronic inflammation of the sinuses; often occurs in clusters; may grow to obstruct nasal breathing and impair the sense of smell

**primary ciliary dyskinesia (PCD):** inherited disorder that prevents cilia from beating properly, causing mucus to build up in the sinuses; also known as immotile-cilia syndrome or Kartagener's syndrome

**pseudoephedrine:** active ingredient in oral decongestants

**pus:** liquid containing white blood cells that forms in response to an infection; often occurs as thick yellow or green drainage during a sinus infection

**quinolones:** powerful class of antibiotic that may be used for persistent sinus infections

**radiofrequency turbinate reduction:** technique used to reduce the size of an enlarged turbinate by delivering a measured amount of heat energy through a specialized needle probe into the turbinate tissue

**rebound:** phenomenon in which symptoms return following cessation of a treatment; often occurs with prolonged use of over-the-counter decongestant nasal sprays for congestion

**reflux:** see *gastroesophageal reflux disease* and *laryngopharyngeal reflux*

**revision surgery:** surgery performed as a follow-up to initial surgery

**rhinitis:** inflammation of the mucous membranes of the nose

**rhinosinusitis:** inflammation of the nose and sinuses; used synonymously with *sinusitis*

**Samter's triad:** see *triad asthma*

**sarcoidosis:** disease characterized by the formation of small beadlike patches of inflamed cells known as granulomas throughout the body, particularly the lungs; may cause sinusitis

**septal perforation:** hole in the nasal septum; can be caused by septoplasty, nasal trauma, or diseases such as Wegener's granulomatosis; can lead to excessive crust formation and bleeding

**septoplasty:** surgery to straighten a deviated nasal septum

**septum:** see *nasal septum*

**shaver:** see *microdebrider*

**sick building syndrome:** set of symptoms (such as headache, fatigue, eye irritation, breathing difficulties, and sinusitis) that is believed to be caused by indoor pollutants

**silent reflux:** see *laryngopharyngeal reflux*

**sinuses:** air–filled cavities in the bones of the skull and face; most people have four pairs of sinuses

**sinusitis:** inflammation of the sinuses

**sinusitis cycle:** self-perpetuating chain of events (infection → swelling → blockage → infection) that occurs during sinusitis

**Sinusitis Spectrum:** concept used to illustrate the wide range of disorders that can present as sinusitis; divides into three general categories—Locals, Intermediates, and Systemics—based upon the cause and severity of disease

**sinus obliteration:** surgical procedure in which a frontal sinus is eliminated by removing all the interior tissue and filling the cavity with fat from the abdomen

**small–hole technique:** sinus surgery that involves making a limited opening into the ethmoid sinuses; also known as minimally invasive surgical technique (MIST)

**sphenoid sinuses:** sinuses located behind the nose

**steroids:** see *nasal steroids*

**Systemics:** individuals on the Sinusitis Spectrum whose disease is caused by a diffuse or generalized disorder often associated with illnesses affecting other areas of their bodies as well, such as asthma

**triad asthma:** a cause of chronic sinusitis characterized by three problems: asthma, aspirin sensitivity, and nasal polyps; also known as Samter's triad or aspirin-induced asthma

**turbinates:** scroll–shaped bones inside the nose covered by mucous membranes that play a key role in conditioning inhaled air before it reaches the lungs; there are three pairs of turbinates: the inferior, middle, and superior

**turbinectomy:** surgical procedure in which a portion of a turbinate bone and/or the surrounding mucous membrane is removed

**vacuum sinusitis:** form of sinusitis in which the interior lining of an obstructed sinus absorbs oxygen, causing negative pressure within the sinus and pain to occur

**Wegener's granulomatosis:** disease that causes formation of granulomas in the sinuses, lungs, and kidneys; associated tissue damage can cause chronic sinusitis and result in septal perforation

# Additional Resources

| Organization | Provides Information On | Website |
|---|---|---|
| American Academy of Otolaryngology | Finding an ENT specialist in your area, as well as ear, nose, and throat topics, including sinusitis | entnet.org |
| American Rhinologic Society | Nasal and sinus topics | american-rhinologic.org |
| American Academy of Allergy, Asthma, and Immunology | Allergy issues related to sinusitis | aaaai.org |
| National Institute of Allergy and Infectious Diseases | Allergy and infection issues related to sinusitis | niaid.nih.gov |
| InteliHealth | General health and disease topics, including sinusitis | intelihealth.com |
| American Herbal Products Association | Herbal supplements for sinusitis | ahpa.org |
| U.S. Environmental Protection Agency | Sick building syndrome as a possible cause of sinusitis | epa.gov/iaq/whereyoulive.html |
| U.S. Food and Drug Administration | Health-related news, including drug and device safety related to sinusitis | fda.gov |
| PubMed Central (U.S. National Library of Medicine) | Scientific research, including abstracts of published studies on sinusitis | pubmedcentral.nih.gov |

# Index

Protein, 29
Proton pump inhibitors, 178
Protonix, 178
Pseudoephedrine, 82, 196
*Pseudomonas*, 100
PubMed Central (U.S. National Library of Medicine), 201
Purulent mucus, 29
Pus, 29, 156, 196

Qi, 117
Quality of life issues, 3–10
Quinolones, 101, 102, 197

Rabago, David, 66
Radioallergosorbent tests (RAST), 44, 110
Radiofrequency turbinate reduction, 197
RAST. *See* Radioallergosorbent tests (RAST)
Rebound, 197
Reflux, 177–78, 197
*Relaxation Response, The* (Benson), 120
Revision surgery. *See* Surgery
Rhinitis, 197
Rhinocort Aqua, 93
Rhinosinusitis, 197
Rhinovirus, 48
Robotic surgery, 185–86
Roosevelt, Franklin Delano, 6

Saline solutions, 70
Saline sprays, 76, 78–79
Samter's triad. *See* Triad asthma
Sarcoidosis, 172–73, 197
Schneiderian membrane, 44
Septal perforation, 197
Septoplasty, 197
Septum, 11, 195. *See also* Deviated septum
Shaver. *See* Microdebriders
Shellfish, 110
Sick building syndrome, 109, 197–98
  workplace issues, 113

Sick cubicle syndrome, 114
Silent reflux. *See* Laryngopharyngeal reflux (LPR)
Sinu-Free, 120
Sinus obliteration, 198. *See also* Surgery
Sinus tumors, 166–67
Sinuses, 25–33, 198
  anatomy, 11–24
  before and after surgery, 137
  at birth, 19
  cysts, 40
  function of, 25
  lining, 20
  theories of function, 21–23
Sinusitis, 198
  acute, 9, 47–53, 189
  anatomical causes, 26
  blockage, 26–33, 39
  children and, 169–71
  chronic, 4
  definition, 5
  disorders that mimic, 177–82
  duration of infection and surgery, 126
  environmental, 26
  frequency of infection and surgery, 125
  fungal, 153–57
  genetic, 26, 171–72
  history of, 40–41
  intermediates, 55, 58, 59–60, 92, 127, 186, 193
  locals, 55–57, 58, 92, 127, 193
  during pregnancy, 171
  quality of life issues, 3–10
  role for fungi, 156–57. *See also* Sinusitis, fungal
  spectrum, 55–62, 92, 127, 128, 186, 198
  symptoms, 30–33, 36, 97–98
  systemics, 55, 57–59, 92, 127, 186, 198
Sinusitis, acute, 9, 47–53, 189
  easing symptoms, 49
  medications, 50–53
  time frame, 47